MW00942155

Denied Entry

A Survivor's Journey
of Fate, Faith and Freedom

Philip S. Freund
Co-Author Belle Anne Freund

Remember the past
Live in the present
Plan for the future

Belle Anne Freund

© 2011 Philip S. Freund

Cover Art by Philip A. Freund

ISBN-13: 978-1456351489

Contents

Foreward

On May 13, 1939, the MS St. Louis set sail from Hamburg, Germany, to cross the Atlantic Ocean with 937 German Jews. They were innocent, frightened men, women and children, seeking asylum in Cuba before immigrating to the United States.

Philip S. Freund was one of the passengers on this historic ship. He celebrated his eighth birthday on June 5, while on the ship, in Cuban waters. This is the story of the events that involved him and his family before, during, and after this tragic voyage, an important event in history that altered the course of European Jewry.

Philip has narrated these events over a span of twenty years.

The lessons we wish to pass on to our readers are these:

NEVER FORGET the past, but learn from it.
Move on and be optimistic about your future.
Do not give up.
Stick with what you believe in.
Do the best job you can to have a fulfilling life.
Always remember to show your gratitude by helping others.
We only live once, so make each day count.

BELLE ANNE FREUND
MENOMONEE FALLS, WI

Dedication

———— ⊱•◊•⊰ ————

This book is dedicated to my parents, Max Joseph Freund, and Theresa Freund. My father died a true hero. He forfeited his life in order to save his wife and children from annihilation. He was a true patriot. My mother, Theresa Freund, nee Lauchheimer, eventually Thea Herz, had the courage and strength to bring four of us out of Germany before it was too late. She saved herself, my grandmother, Ida Lauchheimer, my sister, Liselotte, and myself from the death camps.

My mother and family went from riches to rags when we arrived in the United States without a cent to our names. She went to work in the garment industry sewing collars on t-shirts earning twenty-five cents an hour. She also sold chocolates from door to door. Grandma Ida went to work cleaning people's homes. We lived on the fourth floor of a cold-water tenement in Manhattan.

When my mother remarried in 1951 and came to Milwaukee, she continued to work in the garment industry. Later, William B. Herz, her second husband, opened a Laundromat and she washed other people's dirty clothes. Truly, she was "A Woman of Valor".

I also dedicate this book to my wife, Belle Anne, whose determination and writing skills made this project possible. She has been my mentor, guiding light, staunchest supporter, best friend and motivator. I would never have reached my level of success without her support. She is truly a great "Woman of Valor" and I love her with all my heart and soul.

The purpose of this book is to inform future generations of the trials and tribulations that I overcame, and so that the unanswerable questions can be answered.

— PHILIP S. FREUND

Appreciation

Throughout my life there have been many people who have contributed to my welfare and successes. I appreciate their interests and thank them wholeheartedly. If I have missed anyone here, it is unintentional and I apologize.

First I want to thank Belle Anne who has always stood by me and encouraged me to follow my dreams. One of her dreams was to complete this book. We did it by using her persuasion the whole way. I love her with all my heart and soul.

In spite of the tragedies in her life, my mother, Thea, had the strength and determination to save me from the Nazi's. Even though she went from "riches to rags ", she brought us to the United States where we could live a free life. In her later years she received much pleasure from our children, her grandchildren: Margarette, Mark, Perry and Jacqueline.

Our children and their families, Mark, Laura and Philip, Jacqueline, Craig, Joseph, Samuel, and Daniel, have stood by us through illnesses, good health, and needs, and we have shared many experiences together. They have encouraged us in so many ways. Some have even taken the time to help edit this book.

George Codi, my second to seventh grade mentor, introduced me to literature and a thirst for knowledge.

Lt Robert Vernon saved my life during Basic Training at Camp Atterbury, Indiana, when I could have drowned.

Dan Kriplean, a Whitefish Bay Policeman, accepted me as a volunteer auxiliary, and usually spent nine hours a week with me in his squad car, protecting the citizens of Whitefish Bay,WI. Needless to say, we solved the world's problems during those hours.

Ed Brown was our best man at our wedding, and my close friend in High School in New York. Along with Sandy Berghoffen, they and their families contributed to my sanity while I lived in New York.

COL Bert Handwork influenced my military career by directing my education for future promotions. The requirement that I needed to be a native born American was waived because of Bert's efforts. I was the first naturalized American to work in the office of HQS INSCOM (Headquarters Intelligence and Security Command), the Army element to the National Security agency). I was in that position for sixteen years.

Aunt Edith and Uncle Werner gave me a home from 1939 to 1946 so that I would not go into foster care and live with strangers. My mother could not afford to care for me when she moved to New York City in 1940.

Madi and Werner Blank were kind people who always had a warm meal for me, as well as used clothing that they received from their friends.

A special thank you to Laura, our daughter-in-law, who agreed to handle the publishing process of this book. Belle Anne was overwhelmed with this project and Laura took over with heart and soul.

This book is our contribution to help future generations of our family understand my past and appreciate this great country.

Read, work hard, never give up, so that your dreams become a reality.

— PHILIP S. FREUND

Acknowledgements

———————— ⪧◆⪦ ————————

I thank my husband, Phil, for dictating his life adventure's to me for so many years. It was not easy to remember the unpleasantness of the past. I have attempted to write most of this book in his words. I appreciate his patience. We needed to do this for all our future generations.

I also thank our children, Mark and Jacqueline, who traveled along with us to many of the reunions of the survivors of the voyage of the MS St. Louis. They have supported us every step of the journey.

When Laura Freund, Mark's wife, offered to take over formatting and publishing this book, she relieved me of a great burden. We owe our thanks to her, for without her help this story might not be available.

Thank you to all our friends and acquaintances that supported us when we discussed this book. Thank you to my tutors at the Apple Computer Retail Store, in the Mayfair Shopping Center in Wauwatosa, WI who taught me so much about the use of the computer and were always interested in hearing about the progress of our book.

Thank you to Mark, Jacqueline, and Joseph, our grandson, for helpful suggestions when proofreading this work.

Finally, thank you to Diane Forman for her encouragement to continue working on this project. She was very helpful.

In December, 2009, after the 70 year reunion of the MS St. Louis survivors in Miami, I realized the time had come to complete this project. Other survivors had written their stories, so it was time for me to help Phil complete his.

— BELLE ANNE FREUND

Biographical Roster

RESIDENCES
1931-1939 Munich, Germany
1939-1946 Hackensack, New Jersey
1946-1951 New York City
1951-1954 Active Duty – Army
1954-1995 Milwaukee, WI
1995-date Menomonee Falls, WI

MILITARY PROMOTIONS
PFC 1951
CPL 1952
SSG 1955
SFC 1956
First SGT 1957
First LT 1960
CPT 1963
MAJ 1970
LTC 1974
COL 1983

MILITARY EDUCATION
Orientation Course – MI
Advanced Course – MI
Career Course – MI
Command and General Staff – 1970
Industrial College – Armed Forces – 1974
War College – 1976
Logistical Management – 1980

MILITARY UNITS
103 Engr Bn 28 ID – 1951-1954
309 Engr Bn 84 ID – 1954-1956
643 MI Det – 1956-1963
5063 US Garrison – 1963-1965
HQS 5A – 1965-1970
424 MI Det (Strat) – 1970-1975
HQS INSCOM – 1975-1991
5US Army Area Intel School – 1960-1982

CIVILIAN EDUCATION
George Washington High School – 1950
NYU – 1950
UWM 1954-1957 BA
Marquette U 1966 MEd

CIVILIAN POSITIONS
Oak Creek MS, WI – 1959-1960
Milwaukee Public Schools – 1960-1990
Whitnall MS, WI – 1991-1994
Aux Whitefish Bay PD, WI – 1993-2008

Hollywood Version of the MS St. Louis

In 1978, while stationed in Washington DC, my commanding officer asked me if I had a copy of the movie the MS St. Louis, Hollywood version. When I replied "no", he informed me as to how to get a copy. I was to call the Library of Congress to determine who owned the rights of this film. I was then to request a copy from the owner.

When I called the gentleman, and made my request known, he asked me why I wanted this film. When I told him that I was aboard the St. Louis in 1939, he was amazed, especially when I told him that now I was a Colonel in the US Army.

I asked him what the cost would be. He replied, "Nothing. This is a gift from a fellow Jew to another". Eventually it came on a cassette to me in the mail. We were thankful that he sent us a copy.

NEVER FORGET is our motto.

PHILIP S. FREUND
COL (RET) USA

Denied Entry

The time had come to leave our home.
To start our travels and then to roam.
We traveled on for 40 days and 40 nights;
We felt like sheep, we had no rights.

The call of Miami Beach was there;
We had to leave, it was not fair.
Cuba had said no to us, so few;
The time would come, this day they'd rue.

Because of them so many died;
They made a promise, then they lied.
The blood of many is on their hands,
Of all of those who wore Jewish bands.

Now today, the time has come,
That repentance is made to only some.
But what about those who are not here?
Their memory should always be very dear.

Never again, we say loud and clear,
Or this could happen again, we fear.
Never again, to all we will tell,
As we try to mend and be well.

Our dear Christian friends here care so very much,
As they reach out to us with love and touch.
You felt the sins your forbears made,
And learn of the sacrifices, of which we paid.

Whole families were wiped away,
In unmarked graves so many lay.
And many do not have a place of their own,
Where we can mark them with a stone.

So never forget those not here,
The six million Jews – all those so dear.
They paid a price that we may live,
Their memory to our children we continue to give.

We thank you so very much,
For caring about generations lost.
Of the valuable contributions that could have been made,
What a horrible price to have paid.

Who knows what discoveries would be,
What beautiful art that we would see.
Or the music that we would hear,
So lovely that in our eyes would be a tear.

So much lost and for what reason?
It is too late, it is already done.
They made the world so much better,
They followed the rule to the letter.

We cannot imagine the hopelessness they felt;
Those in the camps – with which they dealt.
They prayed to God and went to their fate,
The liberation for many came too late.

937 passengers could have been saved,
Of them the Cubans could have raved.
Then 6 million would not have been killed;
But it was not in the cards – it was not willed.

So, today, at our feet you lay,
But what a horrible price to pay.
Yet we are honored and forgive,
For, because of the others, our life we live.

We will always remember this date,
And thank God for our fate.
To live our lives
For those who died.

— BY BELLE ANNE FREUND

A tribute to my wonderful husband, Philip Freund,
from your loving wife, Belle Anne.
Ft. Lauderdale, Florida, June 5, 2001

Prologue

My mothers' lineage: The Marx Family, traces their history back to living in the Iberian Peninsula, Spain and Portugal, from AD 600 to 1500 along side the Moors or Muslims. The Muslims permitted the Jews to have religious freedom.

The Crusades from 1000 to 1300 had little impact upon the Jews living in Spain. When the Moors were defeated in 1492, the inquisition was initiated to rid the Iberian Peninsula of all non–Catholics.

The Muslims granted the Jews religious freedom until they were driven out of Spain. The church and the new government questioned the people's beliefs.

King Ferdinand and Queen Isabella wanted a Catholic country. Once it was promulgated, non-Catholics were given three choices: stay and be baptized, leave the country, or be burned at the stake. The Crusades created discrimination against the Jews.

Some Jews were baptized because they wanted to stay in Spain. They secretly kept some traditions. Known as Crypto Jews, they lit Sabbath candles and the Hanukah Menorah and they kept the Passover, in their own interpretation. They spoke Ladino rather than Yiddish. In time, the next generation would not remember why they had these traditions, but still continued to practice them.

Most Jews left Spain for religious freedom. The Marx ancestors walked to Southern Germany and settled in the smaller towns.

During the Thirty Year War, from 1618 to 1648, the Lutherans invaded Southern Germany and attacked the fortified cities. The Marx family lived in Bavaria in small agriculturally based villages, like Pflaumloch and Lauchheim, from 1500 until the conclusion of the Thirty Year War.

The Marx family was allowed to seek refuge inside the fortified cities and was protected from the invaders. Up to that time they lived safely outside of these cities.

At the termination of the war they were allowed to become permanent residents of the fortified cities including Rothenburg and Noerdlingen.

By 1810, Napoleon had overrun Europe. He eliminated the Jewish ghettos, as he believed in Liberty, Equality, and Fraternity. Jews were allowed to assimilate into society with the general population. Jews and Muslims were accepted by Napoleon, but were not permitted to participate in governmental affairs.

Over the centuries, my family became true Germans. They were assimilated into German society because they found a country where they were accepted and safe. They were more proud to be Bavarian than German.

My mothers' mother; Grandma Ida Marx, and her ten siblings lived in the fortified city, Noerdlingen. The Marx family home in Noerdlingen still stands. On the first floor of the yellow house is Daniel's Café. In front of the house stands a water fountain with a statue of a soldier in the middle. On it is inscribed "Erected in memory of those Jewish soldiers who fought in the Franco-Prussian War of 1872".

In 1870, Germany was made up of many small states which were controlled by a royal family, the church, or a combination of the two. All these states had different dialects, which resulted in Germans having difficulty in communicating. Even today in the small towns the different dialects continue to represent the specific areas.

Otto von Bismarck wished to unify the states into one Germany. Being the Chancellor of Prussia, he had the support of the Kaiser, to create a plan to unite the country. He sent a telegram to France that was insulting to the French. The French wrote back an insulting letter to Bismarck.

Bismarck wanted this to instigate a war which would result in the unification of Germany. He published this letter from the French in the German newspaper, and the German people were outraged.

United in anger, the Germans formed an army and marched into France. They besieged Paris and cut off the cities supplies. The people were so desperate; they even resorted to consuming their house pets since food was blocked from entering the city. Paris surrendered to Germany in 1872.

The resulting peace treaty forced the French to give up the Rhineland, which had become a heavy industrial area with coal and iron ore mines. This allowed Germany to build up their industrial capability.

In the late 1880's, the Germans realized that France and England controlled colonies in Africa. Germany needed the natural resources, which Africa had to offer, so colonies were established there.

In order to have peace in Europe, alliances were established between groups of countries called the "Balance of Power". France, England and Russia were on one side. Russia included Russia, Poland, Latvia, Lithuania, and Estonia. On the other side were Germany, and the Austro-Hungarian Empire, that included Czechoslovakia, Serbia, Croatia, Hungary, Romania and Bulgaria. It was a well balanced arrangement.

In 1914 Archduke Ferdinand and his wife Sophia, of the Austro-Hungarian Empire, went on a good will tour in Sarajevo, Serbia. The nationalists in Serbia wanted independence. Ferdinand and Sophia were assassinated by Princip, a Serbian, who shot them while they were riding in their car. The car with the bullet holes is in the Schoenbrunn Castle- a museum in Vienna, Austria.

Ferdinand was the son of Franz Joseph, the Emperor of Austria, the Austro-Hungarian Empire, who also was the nephew of Queen Victoria, of England. Nicolas, the Czar of Russia, was related to Queen Victoria, as was Kaiser Wilhelm, who came from the house of Windsor and they were all originally German.

Franz Josef wanted to punish the Serbs for the assassination, but Russia had a treaty with the Serbs and came to their aid. The Germans were allied with the Austro-Hungarian Empire and the Russians were allied with Serbia, France and England. Because of the assassination of Archduke Ferdinand the Balance of Power ceased to exist; WWI was initiated.

Lenin was living in neutral Switzerland in 1914, when WWI broke out, because he was exiled from Russia for his revolutionary ideas. Germany did not want Russia participating in the war. Lenin was secretly placed by the Germans in a sealed train and sent back to Russia with the political goal of fermenting unrest and overthrowing the Czarist government.

Lenin arrived in St. Petersburg, in October of 1917, to start a revolution with his many followers who considered him an icon. Russia stayed out of the war by suing for peace and signing the Treaty of Brest Litovsk. As a result, Russia had to forfeit the territories of Poland, Lithuania, Latvia and Estonia.

Meanwhile Germany had many casualties in the trenches of France.

In 1918, the US intervened in the war to help the French and English defeat Germany, after the Germans sank a US ship, the MS Lusitania that was carrying war supplies to England.

The war ended November 11, 1919. Germany lost.

Germany was blamed for the war and as a result was forced to pay billions of marks of reparations to Poland and France. The German army was reduced to 100,000 men. Germany also was forced to give up territory. Austria was split into Austria and Hungary. The treaty of Versailles stripped Germany of land, the Rhineland, Memel, and Danzik which established Yugoslavia, Czechoslovakia and Poland.

There were communists and fascists in Germany. Rosa Luxemburg, who was Jewish, was a proponent of a communist state in Germany. The Monarchists, Socialists, and Democrats were against communism; there were lots of public protests and social unrest.

The Weinmar Republic was a democracy, but could not control the country because there was a great amount of internal conflict. It did not have the majority support in its legislature. The Republic dissolved the parliament and called for new elections.

The National Socialist German Workers Party was a strong movement. This organization was highly anti-Semitic. When the war was over and the soldiers were discharged there were no jobs. Inflation was raging. People were hungry. EVERYONE WAS REALLY ANGRY.

Hitler was in the German Army, and at the conclusion of the war, was sent to Munich. He served under Field Marshal Eric Ludendorf, who was in charge of the army.

Hitler came from Braunau, Austria, where he lived with his mother, Klara, and his stepfather. He wanted to become a famous artist and applied to an exclusive Art Academy. His application was rejected. He blamed the Jewish members of the board for turning him down as a student.

Hitler fought in France during WWI. He was gassed and temporarily blinded. He was in the First Company, Sixteenth Infantry Regiment. His Commander was LTC Philipp Engelhardt, his Platoon Leader was First Lieutenant Fritz Weedemann and his company Commander, a Jew, was Captain Gutman.

His Jewish company commander decorated Hitler for bravery. Unfortunately, Hitler's mother had a Jewish doctor who treated her for cancer by putting acid on her cancer sores, which caused her death. Hitler was very close to his mother. He felt that the Jews were to blame for all his woes.

After WWI, the Freikorps was formed by Captain Roehm to bring stability to Germany. The Freikorps was based on fascism. Hitler joined the group and spied on breakaway political groups such as communists, socialists, and monarchists, to gather information for the Freikorps.

Captain Roehm assigned Hitler to attend a meeting of the National Socialist German Workers Party, NSDAP, which eventually became the Nazi Party. The Freikorps were the dregs of society, who lacked morality and were willing to follow any order. They were affiliated with the NSDAP.

Hitler resonated with what he heard: the members hated the Jews and Communists, and thought of themselves as Nationalists and Socialists. They wanted to restore the army beyond limitations imposed by the Versailles Peace Treaty.

Captain Roehm created the SA, the Security Detachment, also known as the Brown Shirts, which later became the SS, to guard Hitler. In 1935 Hitler thought Roehm wanted to take over the Nazi party, so he had all those under Roehm killed. This was known as the "Night of the Long Knives". Before Roehm was killed he told Hitler that he was not a traitor.

Hitler assumed the leadership of the Nazi party and became its speaker. On November 9, 1923, Hitler, Herman Goering and General Ludendorf tried to take over Munich and the Bavarian Government by starting a "Putsch", a coup d'etat, to overthrow the government, but it failed. The SA marched down a street where there was an ambush and some of them were killed.

One of the men, Horst Wessel, became a martyr for the Nazi movement. The rest were arrested and Hitler was sentenced to nine months in Landshut Prison. Rudolph Hess, a college student in Munich who became interested in the Nazis, chose to go to prison with Hitler, as his secretary. Hitler dictated his book: MEIN KAMPF (My Struggle) to Hess during his sentence. The book was well received, it made him wealthy.

Goering was shot in the upper part of his leg and fell in a doorway of an apartment house. Two German ladies took him to the hospital and smuggled him out of the country to Switzerland. Years later he saved these two Jewish ladies by helping them get to Switzerland. Goering was a fighter pilot in WWI. Hitler brought him back to Germany to take part in the new German government. He was made the head of Prussia, around 1920.

The German Parliament elected Hitler as a Representative from Bavaria. He blamed the Jews for losing WWI. Reparations made the country poor and caused unemployment and inflation. He promised the people jobs if he was elected. While in Parliament he wanted to become the Chancellor of Germany. There were splinter parties and Hitler represented the Nazi Party. The party did not gain the majority vote.

In 1933, Hindenburg was President of Germany. The Nazis found out that his son, Oscar, was heavily in debt from gambling and they bought his markers, (gambling IOU's). They threatened to foreclose on the family estate unless Hindenburg appointed Hitler as Chancellor. On his deathbed, in order to restore the dignity of his family and clear his son, Hindenburg appointed Hitler as Chancellor. This is how Hitler came into power.

To consolidate Hitler's hold in the Parliament, Hitler declared extraordinary emergency measures. Goering had a disabled Dutch national set fire to the upper house of the legislature, and Hitler blamed the Communists. Hitler then started the concentration camps and arrested Communists, Socialists, Free Masons, Gypsies and Jews, and others he considered a threat to his government, or people he considered to be inferior and not worthy of German citizenship.

In 1935, in Nurenberg, the legislature passed a racial law that stripped Jews of their citizenship and rights. Jews could no longer hold government jobs. They could not take the role of a plaintiff in court. Their bank accounts were blocked. They could not vote. They could be arrested without a warrant and executed without due process. They lost all of their civil rights. This set the stage for the destruction of European Jewry.

Guns, radios, and binoculars were confiscated from all Jews. The Germans had kept meticulous records and knew who owned these items. Everyone was required to be registered when buying them.

Jews had to get permission from the Gestapo to obtain their own money and then go to the bank to get it. They were allowed only to withdraw a small amount of money, and thus could not buy all the items that were needed, or wanted.

Hitler formed a winter charity and became wealthy from the workers contributions. Everyone who worked was obligated to contribute to this charity. The money was supposed to be redistributed to the unemployed to provide them with food, and clothing. Hitler misappropriated these funds for his own purpose.

Hitler met his companion, Eva Brown when he was sitting for a portrait at a photography studio.

In November of 1938, Greenspan, a Polish Jew killed the German Deputy Ambassador to France. At that time he was living in Paris. His family was expelled from Germany and sent to the polish-German border where they were kept in limbo. His attempt was to kill the German Ambassador, but instead he killed the Deputy Ambassador, who happened to be friendlier to the Jews. The French Police arrested him. When the Germans invaded Paris in 1940 and found him in jail, they executed him. The killing of the Deputy Ambassador led to Kristalnacht.

In 1939, the Cuban government, under President Bru, decided to allow a small number of Jews seeking exile from Nazi Germany to use Cuba as a stop over before immigrating to the United States. The MS St. Louis of the Hamburg American Line had a route between Germany and Havana. Nine hundred and thirty seven Jews purchased round trip tickets on this vessel. Mr. Gonzales, the Cuban representative, collected the fee for the Cuban entry visa. Instead of fulfilling the visa purchase with the Cuban authorities, he pocketed the money, thereby voiding the entry permits.

Hitler knew that Mr. Gonzales absconded the money. He placed Gestapo agents on the ship to create a problem, if necessary, to prevent passengers from disembarking.

Upon arrival in the Havana Harbor, the pro Nazis movement in Cuba held demonstrations to prevent the passengers from disembarking. Hitler used this as proof that no nation was willing to accept Jews.

On September 1, 1939, German troops invaded Poland which commenced World War II.

In 1941, the Wansee Conference was held outside Berlin. The "Final Solution" was established that eventually led to the extermination of six million Jews and six million others.

World War II ended in May of 1945.

Hitler and Eva Brown married right before committing suicide in a bunker in Berlin along with their dog Blondie in 1945.

My Family

MY FATHER, Max Joseph Freund, was born in a Bavarian town called Kleinwaldstadt, "Little Woodsy City", near Aschafenburg, Germany in 1897. He had one brother, Manfred. Their parents, Phillipp and Jenny, died in the early 1920s.

In 1912, at the age of fifteen, my father joined the Kaiser's Army and fought in World War I from 1914 to 1919. He was a platoon leader in the Fifth Infantry Regiment, and was assigned to a heavy weapons company. As a lieutenant in 1915, he single-handedly took out a French pillbox. For this brave deed he was awarded the Iron Cross Third Class, similar to the US Bronze Star. His dream was to be a professional soldier, but he was forced out of the army after Germany lost the war, and the Versailles Treaty reduced the German army to only one hundred thousand men.

In 1900 my maternal grandfather, Siegfried Lauchheimer, founded Becker und Roegel, a printing company, in Munich. Siegfried met my grandmother, Ida Marx, fell in love, and married. They loved Munich because it was a cosmopolitan city, much different from their respective small towns they were raised in. They loved what Munich had to offer: the theatre, the museums and the possibility of meeting many more sophisticated people.

Grandma Ida had four brothers, that I knew of, Herman, Willy, Hugo and Sigmund. Grandpa Siegfried gave Willy and Sigmund important positions in the company. Hugo became president of a bank in Munich. Herman was an ambulance driver in World War I. There was a sister, Sophie. I remember my mother taking me to visit Sophie when she was sick and bedridden. She died a couple of months before Kristalnacht. I never met or heard about Grandma Ida's other seven siblings.

At that time, greeting cards were used by many people. The business also produced advertisements on round columns, called Litfasssaeule, still found in most European cities on the street corners. These columns, made out of metal, are used in place of billboards. They are hollow and have access doors containing supplies, such as glue and the ads that are stored inside until they are pasted on the outside. My family became very wealthy from this business.

In 1906, Siegfried and Ida became parents of twin girls, Theresa and Edith. The twin sisters grew up with all the privileges that wealth could buy., the best clothing, travel, food and upper class acquaintances. They went to the theatre and attended parties with educated people. One of their friends was Hans J. Morganthau, who became a professor at the University of Chicago. He became a friend of Henry Kissinger.

The girls had a very happy childhood. They had many friends since twins were unique in those days, and to the students in school they were a novelty. My mother, Theresa, and Aunt Edith felt very special. They had a very active social life in high school.

When the girls were eighteen years old, Siegfried died from an infection. Grandma Ida was very despondent and mourned for her husband for the rest of her life. Her brothers, Sigmund and Willy, continued to run the business. Until the Nazis took over, Grandma Ida received a pension and her daughters lived with her until they married.

Aunt Edith married a doctor, Werner Gould, from Leipzig, Germany, and they moved to Darmstadt, Hessen, Germany.

My mother met Max Joseph Freund when he began to work for Becker und Roegel. Max was a great salesman and soon became head of the sales department. Later he was promoted to manager of the sales department. It was foreseen that one day he would become president of the firm.

He won my mother's heart and in 1928, they married, at the Hauptsynagogue in Munich.

The good life continued for the young couple as my father was able to provide for every wish of my mother. They attended and hosted parties for their friends, or having afternoon tea or dinner with them. They spent many Sundays walking in the woods.

My mother was always attentive to her mother, and most weekday afternoons the two had afternoon tea together, or shopped or walked to

Marienplatz in the center of Munich by the City Hall, and by the Frauenkirche, The Church of Our Lady. They would stop at one of the cafes for cake or ice cream and coffee.

Soon my parents had a family. I was born June 5, 1931, and Liselotte, my sister, was born November 9, 1934.

Life for us was good. We had a Packard car and a chauffeur, who drove us to the mountains, to our summer home, or to the shops. We had Anna, our cook, and Paula, our governess. When the Nazis took over life slowly began to turn sour.

In the mid-1930s, when anti-Semitism became rampant, many Jews were already starting to flee Germany. The Nazis wanted the country to be "Judenfrei", free of all Jews, and were happy to allow Jews to leave. My father did not want to leave Germany. He was a good soldier and served with distinction, by which he assumed his family would be safe in Germany. He felt that life would return to normal. Many of the Jews felt this was a passing phase.

Because my father held an important position in the company, he often traveled to Sweden and Holland to promote the business. He became a friend of Count Bernadotte of Sweden, with whom he conducted his printing business. By 1935, Count Bernadotte saw what was happening in Germany and offered to set up a printing factory for the company in Stockholm. He wanted my father to leave Germany and seek refuge in Sweden. Being the true German that he was, my father refused the offer. My father had his head in the sand and refused to budge.

When the Nurmberg racial laws were passed in 1935, Uncle Werner realized what was happening and knew he must take his family to safety. He was fortunate to have a distant cousin, Dr. Gordon, living in New Jersey. At that time the United States was in dire need of doctors, and Uncle Werner was willing to settle anywhere. Dr. Gordon urged Uncle Werner to immigrate to the United States, and offered to serve as his sponsor. Uncle Werner applied for visa and quota numbers and Dr. Gordon helped him obtain a priority visa to enter the country. Uncle Werner was able to leave in 1935 and establish a home in Hackensack, New Jersey. Aunt Edith and their son

Arthur followed in 1937 when their quota numbers were called.

My mother begged my father to go with Uncle Werner so that we could join him with Aunt Edith and bring Grandma Ida. She was worried about the safety of all of us. In 1935, my mother registered with the American Consulate for an immigration quota number. Because my father did not have a medical degree, he was unable to leave.

As rights were taken away from the Jews, my father finally realized that we should leave. Knowing he would not be allowed to take his own money out of Germany, his uncles thought that it was easier to export company money. The uncles were the Board of Directors. They decided that my father should take the firms money out of the country in order to establish a branch of the firm in a safer place. My father knew if he was caught, this would be a death sentence. He was trying to save the family and did not expect to get caught.

Early in 1937, on a business trip, my father began to smuggle money to a bank in Amsterdam, Holland. He wanted to use this money to start a branch of the company ultimately in Sweden. Unfortunately, it was too late. The Nazis already began to audit the factory books in Munich and confiscate money. They discovered my father was removing money and they demanded that it be returned.

In order to protect my mother, my father wanted her to know as little as possible. Since the Gestapo knew everything about everyone, it was almost impossible not to be caught. My father knew that my mother would have vehemently objected to what he was doing. In order to locate my father, the Gestapo arrested and interrogated her for hours. She could only tell the Gestapo what she knew, which was not much. She had no knowledge of how the firm functioned. She was shocked to hear what my father had done. She was forced to contact my father and advise him of her arrest.

In October of 1937, my father returned to Germany with the money, and was taken to Dachau, a concentration camp outside of Munich, where his life ended. My mother was held hostage at Gestapo headquarters, waiting for his return. If he did not return the money, she would have suffered greatly. He paid the ultimate price for attempting to save his family, and the family business. The Nazis had achieved their goal, to get the money, and kill my father.

My mother was not immediately released. While the Gestapo held my mother, Grandma Ida, Paula, and Anna took care of my sister and me. No one told us why my mother was away. We were used to her absence when she traveled with my father.

She was still being held captive when Hans Archenhold, a cousin who had worked at the plant, went to the Gestapo to find out why she was not released. He convinced them to release her to his care since she was of no use to them anymore. Hans was related to a well-known astronomer and the Germans named an observatory after him, outside of Berlin. Because of this, the Nazis allowed my mother to leave, and Hans took her home.

Grandma Ida, Paula and Anna had kept my sister and I entertained by playing with us, so as not to miss our mother. My mother did not tell me that our father passed away. I was used to my mother not telling me anything. Paula, informed me, "Your father died." I was devastated. I wanted my father home. I saw how everyone in our house was unhappy, and crying for days. It was very traumatic for all of us.

My mother was beside herself with grief. Since I was not at the funeral, years later Madie Blank informed me that a Gestapo agent had accompanied the sealed casket to ensure that it was not opened before the burial. My mother buried my father in the Jewish cemetery in Munich. She barely made it through the funeral. My mother blamed herself for not insisting that we leave Germany when she thought it was most necessary. My mother could never forgive herself for not being stronger with my father and insisting that she knew better. If only he listened to her, life would have been completely different in the United States. Guilt added to her grief.

At this point my mother, 31 years old in a male-dominated society which was suffering under totalitarian rule in Hitler's Germany, suddenly became solely responsible for her family.

My Earliest Memories

As a little boy in Germany the greatest enjoyment I can remember were our family vacations. In the summer we often traveled to our country home on the shore of Lake Tegernsee. I loved to be in the water, even though I did not know how to swim. The best memories were that of the travels to the beautiful mountains of Austria and Switzerland.

On these outings I always wore my Lederhosen. The suspenders had the Alpine flower Edelweiss, carved out of bone and sewn on the bar across my chest. I wore woolen knee socks, shoes and an alpine hat. I looked like a typical Alpine boy.

We were driven to the foothills of the Bavarian Alps by our chauffeur, who took us to the end of the road in an Alpine village. We boarded a train that took us as far as the tracks would go. My father and I climbed further up the mountains, saw shepherds' huts, and heard the cowbells. We looked for Edelweiss, but we never found any due to its rarity. Sometimes when we walked through the fields, my father hoisted me on his shoulders for a ride.

On one trip, we walked beside a farmer's field. We saw a post that held a small, three- sided wooden shelter. Inside was a figure of Jesus on the cross. My father explained the significance: the cross represented another religion, and the farmers prayed to it in the hopes of having a good crop. Attached to the bottom of the cross was a shelf where the farmers put little crosses and vases filled with water and flowers.

As we walked from one village to another, they were not far apart, we stopped at an Alpine restaurant, where my parents drank coffee and I had my first taste of mineral water. I did not care much for it.

Sometimes, in some of the little villages, musicians would play Alpine music, which I still love to hear. I remember being intrigued by the sound of a zither. The piece that I loved was "Gloria", a famous Bavarian melody.

I always looked forward to these outings, as I really loved the mountains.

It was on one of our trips to the mountains that I first met Madie and Werner Blank. They lived in Berlin, but had met my parents through mutual acquaintances, and became lifelong friends. Werner was a judge in the lower court. When we went to our country home, the Blank's often spent weekends with us there, as well as weeks when they had longer vacations. From our house, we crossed the street and climbed down steps that led to the sandy beach. My mother was scared to death of water, so I often went with Madie. We played with my toys that I floated on the water. One was a yellow duck. Once when Werner was with us, he waved his hand in front of my face, and I bit his finger. He enjoyed teasing me about that years later.

We lived at 29 Elizabethstrasse in Munich, in a stucco building. The building had four floors, with two homes on each floor. We owned our residence on the second floor. It had large rooms, and off the kitchen was a small balcony. There were extra bedrooms for our live-in help, Anna, the cook, and Gertrude, the maid. Paula, our governess, came every day. Our butler, who was also our chauffeur, did not live with us. We lived a luxurious life.

Grandma Ida lived around the corner on Tenkstrasse and the streetcar ran in front of her house. My mother had tea most afternoons with her, usually at our home, our "wohnung" after 1935. Occasionally, I would join my mother and visit Grandma Ida. On our way to grandma's house, if a Nazi party member wearing a red arm band and a black swastika approached us, we had to step aside, off the sidewalk and into the gutter, to let him pass.

At grandma's apartment, I stood by the window, pushed the curtains aside, and watched the traffic go by in the street. I watched people walk by on the sidewalk. Several high-backed chairs stood close to the windows and I ran my hand on the rough upholstery. I liked the feel of the material. Next to the window was a little table, which I once moved, causing Grandma Ida to become very upset with me. Heavy drapes over the windows made the room very dark. It was boring to visit Grandma Ida because all I did was look out the window while she and my mother talked.

St. Joseph Catholic Church was a few blocks away from our house.

On Christmas Eve, 1937, Paula took me there and I saw a Crèche for the first time. I was amazed. Tiny, perfect figures about four inches high depicted the life of Jesus. They were arranged in several different scenes in a glass showcase along the wall of the church. They were colorful and had captured my attention. I'd never seen anything like this, and I stood for a long time looking at the different scenes. This was different than what I saw in the farmer's field up in the mountains.

The kind priest gave me something that was completely new to me. I was going to take a bite, but he stopped me and told me how to peel it. Paula peeled it for me and I tasted the wonderful flavor of an orange for the first time.

When my father traveled to Sweden on a business trip, he once brought back a huge tub of butter and a wheel of Swiss cheese. This was my first exposure to such delicacies. I continue to enjoy these foods today.

Once a pigeon flew into our kitchen from the balcony and I tried to help Anna capture it. I suggested that it would make a nice stew. Needless to say, I was outvoted.

In the neighborhood near our house was a military garrison. From my window, I could watch the German army march down the street, accompanied by the military marching band. Whenever I heard the band, I too marched in time to the music. Every Sunday the band presented concerts in the English Gardens.

Once in a while, Paula took me to Uncle Herman's house; he lived a block away. He read to me the newspaper about the Spanish Civil War. He also read to me the news about the Graf Zeppelin blowing up in Lakehurst, New Jersey in 1938. When it was safe, Paula and Uncle Herman took me for walks along the Isar River.

Our lives completely changed in 1935, when the Nazis assumed control of every German's life. The "racial laws" took away nearly all our rights. All adult Jews had a "J" stamped on their ID cards and were given middle names, Sarah and Israel. The Jews were considered a lesser class than the rest of the population.

The racial laws restricted every aspect of our lives. Jews could no longer go to the theatre or the movies, ride the streetcar, or play in the park. I always enjoyed going to the park with Paula and did not understand why we were not allowed anymore. From 1935 to November 9, 1938, we were only allowed to walk through the park on the main road, but could not stop to listen to the music.

The Nazis eventually took from the Jews automobiles, shortwave radios, guns, binoculars, and the opportunity to travel. The Nazis took our car and our summer home, ending the wonderful vacations. We became prisoners in our own home. Jews were not allowed to socialize or engage in business with non-Jews.

Jews were put on half-rations for food so I was always hungry. Each family was issued ration books, but half the pages were removed from the books given to the Jews. My mother was well liked by the butcher at "Dahlmeyer's Deli". Before the racial laws took effect, I would go to Dahlmeyer's with my mother and the butcher would give me a slice of salami to eat while my mother did her shopping. Now, we could not ride the street-cars, and it was a long and dangerous walk to that part of Munich so my mother had to shop closer to our home. The neighborhood butcher was kind to my mother and often gave her extra meat.

The Gestapo froze every Jew's bank accounts. In order to get money for groceries, my mother and grandmother had to go to the Gestapo and beg for their own money. There, they would be victims of verbal abuse. They received just enough money for necessities approved by the Nazis, mainly food, toiletries and funds to pay the help.

Since it was difficult to make friends to play with, I mostly played alone. I had a train and a stuffed monkey that were my favorite toys. Sometimes Paula played with me when she was not occupied with my sister.

Because no one took the time to explain our situation I did not understand what was going on in our lives. I felt anger, rejection, bewilderment and fear. I was a scared and lonely boy.

Kristallnacht

IN THE FALL OF 1937, at the age of six, I started out attending a regular German elementary school but being Jewish, I was soon forced to leave. I was later enrolled in a school that the Jewish Community of Munich was allowed to open.

I had no friends or playmates in the neighborhood. I was too young to go outside by myself, and it was too dangerous for Paula, my nanny, to take me to the park. Hitler Youth roamed the streets, looking for innocent Jews to taunt. Once in a while my mother took me outside in the backyard where it was safe.

It was a while before anyone could speak to me about my father. My mother, grandmother, nanny, and the cook, were going through their own grief and they left me alone. My mother was in bed for weeks, mourning for my father. She missed her husband so much that she did not want to live anymore.

My mother's grief had disabled her. She could not look after the family. She had a difficult time realizing that she would never see my father again. My mother believed that the results of her actions had led to my father being turned over to the Gestapo, and her feelings of guilt were unbearable and long lasting. Grandma Ida came every day to care for my mother.

Paula took care of my three-year-old sister and left me to play alone most of the time. The train set and stuffed monkey were birthday presents from my mother. I played with them in an alcove near our front door. I had many other toys but I do not remember what they were.

Slowly my mother began to realize she had to take care of us. She realized that we depended on her. After several weeks in bed, she was able to get up and regain control of her life again. She had to be strong and find a way to get us to safety out of Germany.

On November 9, 1938, two weeks after I entered the Jewish school, the Nazis went on a rampage, smashing the chandeliers in synagogues and the windows of Jewish-owned homes and businesses and looting them. The Nazis threw Torahs into the streets, trampled on the holy books, and desecrated them. They destroyed more than three hundred synagogues setting them on fire.

Firemen and policemen were ordered, "Do not interfere! Do not help the Jews." They stood by and watched the madmen destroy Jewish property. The Gestapo attacked people trying to protect their homes, businesses, and places of worship. No one helped the Jews. That terrible night, November 9, 1938, became known as "Kristallnacht", the "Night of the Broken Glass". All over Germany and Austria, the Nazis destroyed Jewish life and property. My Jewish school was burned to the ground.

That night, all Jewish males over the age of sixteen were arrested and sent to a concentration camp. This round up included two of our family friends, Cantor Hohenemser and Rabbi Baerwalt. They were sent to the nearest concentration camp in a suburb of Munich: Dachau.

That night our family was home hearing noises outside but without any idea of what was happening around us. While playing with my train and monkey I heard a loud knock at the door. I was hoping to see my Grandma Ida. Instead, when I opened the door, I saw two big black boots. I looked up the boots to the knees and onto the black leather coat of a Gestapo agent in uniform. He ordered me to get my father. When I told him that my father was dead, the Gestapo agent kicked me across the room and was ready to stomp on me when my mother ran into the room, demanding to know why her boy was being kicked. She ran to the cabinet by the front door and produced my father's death certificate from the drawer. With that he left.

My mother was very upset at the appearance of the Gestapo agent in her house. As soon as he left, my mother made two phone calls. First she called Lotte Schlumberger, her childhood Catholic friend. Lotte said she would come immediately with her car and driver.

Next, my mother called my father's platoon sergeant from the First World War. He told us to come to his farm, he would protect us. If he was caught, his family would be killed, his animals slaughtered, and his farm burned down. This man held great admiration for my father and was willing to put his family in danger for us. My father looked after him during the war. Now he had a chance to repay him.

My mother packed for us and her mother. She sent her maid across the street to Grandma Ida's home to collect a few items for the trip.

When Lotte arrived, we brought our luggage down to the street where the car was waiting. The driver packed the trunk and we were on our way to the sergeant's farm. My mother trusted her cook and maid to look after the house, until we could return. She hoped that no one would loot our home, while we were gone.

We stayed at the farm more than a week. The farmer took me out in the field to pick sugar beets. I wore a big, floppy, hat so the neighbors would not recognize me as a Jewish boy. The farmer told me stories about my father and what a great soldier he was. I was excited to know that my father had been a hero.

The women stayed inside the farmhouse. Even with the ever-present smell of cattle, the warmth of the animals rising from the lower level kept everyone comfortable. When the chores were completed, and the evening meal was over, I went to bed. The adults listened to news about Munich on the farmer's radio.

Periodically my mother called home to Anna, who reported the current situation. After ten days Anna suggested that we return to the city because there were no reports of attacks on Jews. Life in Munich seemed to have returned to normal. My mother and Grandma Ida were anxious to go back home.

In Germany, everyone over the age of sixteen was required to carry an ID document, similar to a passport. My family's IDs listed their nationality as Bayerish or Bavarian because they lived in Munich, the capital of Bavaria. Until 1872, when it became a part of Germany, this area was a separate country. My grandmother was particularly proud of this heritage and often said to me, "I'm not German—I'm Bavarian!" An addition to the identification card after 1935 was a religious designation: J for Jewish and new middle names for women, Sarah, and men, Israel.

Lotte had been so helpful to take the family to the farm, but my mother did not want to put her in danger by asking her to bring us back. By then, Jews were no longer allowed to travel by train. Yet, somehow my mother was able to purchase train tickets. Possibly the stationmaster was not aware of the regulation governing Jewish travel. If the Nazis found out, he would be punished because he sold her the tickets. We arrived safely back in Munich.

When we returned from the farm, my mother was more determined than ever to leave Germany. Over the next few months we lived a life of high anxiety. We lived a day-to-day existence, never knowing what new regulations would be imposed upon us.

In January 1939, Cantor Hohenemser was released from the camp. He was able to gain release because he had the means to leave Germany. He came to our house. He had been in confinement and was never allowed to bathe, brush his teeth, or change his clothes. After he bathed, my mother showed me how dirty the bathtub was. My mother gave him some of my father's clothes. He was able to immigrate to a synagogue in Rhode Island where the members had sponsored him and helped him get established.

That same month, my mother heard about a ship called the MS St. Louis that was leaving Germany for Cuba. She found out that the Cuban government was willing to accept Jews fleeing the Nazis. It would take 937 Jewish passengers.

Because my mother had registered in 1935, with the American Consulate for an immigration quota number, we were able to leave Germany. She contacted the Cuban litigation in Munich and purchased four visas from Mr. Gonzales. They cost $500 each. Without these entry permits, we would not be able to enter Cuba.

She contacted the Hamburg American Line to purchase four tickets on the MS St. Louis. Even though we would not return to Germany, Jews had to buy roundtrip tickets. Our plan was to go to Cuba and wait for our quota numbers to come up. Then we would immigrate to the US where Aunt Edith and Uncle Werner would be waiting for us. Uncle Werner was now a dermatologist in Hackensack, New Jersey. We were eager to see the family and settle into a new life in the United States.

My mother went to the Gestapo and asked for her own money to purchase tickets to Cuba. The Gestapo gave her enough money for first-class tickets for her, Grandma Ida, my sister, and myself. My mother also had to pay a large exit tax. The Nazis told her if we returned to Germany, we would immediately go to the concentration camp. The Nazis were glad to see Jews leave. Our departure date was May 13, 1939.

Passengers were allowed to take only two suitcases and ten marks, $4.20. That meant that each individual would carry two suitcases. My mother packed clothes suitable for the tropics, as it would be warm and humid in Cuba.

I had to carry my two suitcases. I left most of my clothes behind. My train set stayed behind, as well as most of my toys. I took my stuffed monkey.

Harder than packing our clothes, was leaving everything else behind. My parents had so many possessions. Before Kristallnacht, the Gestapo did not check packages shipped out of the country by Jews. My mother sent some of our belongings to Hackensack with Aunt Edith. She sent some pieces of furniture, that we use today. Jewelry hidden in the linens were packed in large wooden crates. They made it safely to the US.

Of course, we had to leave behind furniture, clothes, jewelry, dishes, and crystal. Some Nazi family would move into our fully furnished home. The Gestapo would take over all the money we left behind. If my mother tried to smuggle her valuables out in a suitcase, she would be shot. What choice did she have? She could not take that chance.

As we made preparations to leave, Grandma Ida refused to pack. In 1937, when Grandma Ida's brothers, Willie, Hugo and Sigmund, were making preparations to leave, they told Ida and their brother Herman to stay in Germany. Herman had a disability and had insufficient funds. The brothers were certain that women, children, and handicapped people were safe to stay in Germany. Ida believed them. Besides, her ancestors lived in Bavaria for hundreds of years, and she lived in Bavaria all her life. Bavaria was her home and no harm would befall her. She was adamant about staying.

We learned later that the first to be killed were people with disabilities, which included Uncle Herman.

My mother insisted that Grandma Ida pack her suitcases, or Anna would go to her home to pack for her. Reluctantly, Grandma Ida prepared to leave. Someone else would enjoy her home, her furnishings, and her money.

We planned to leave Munich for the port in Hamburg on May 11, 1939. I had anxieties about leaving my home, my bed and my belongings.

Going to a strange place was frightening for me, a seven-year-old boy. The only familiar words were Onkel Werner, Tante Edith, and Kusin Arthur. My mother was preoccupied with her own thoughts and had very little time for her children.

Grandma Ida was approachable. I could talk to her, but it was difficult for her to explain what was going on, and she did not understand what the future held.

Cuba would be a temporary stopover prior to our immigrating to the United States.

We could not speak Spanish or English, and had no idea how we would communicate with the Cubans and where we would stay.

For now, our main concern was boarding the ship and leaving Germany.

Departure

WE BOARDED THE TRAIN at the main railroad station in Munich, the Hauptbahnhoff, in the afternoon of May 11, 1939. Gestapo agents were there, watching our every move. When I saw their uniform, I was afraid they might not let us depart.

Because she could not take much money out of the country, my mother had requested sufficient funds to make our trip comfortable. For our trip to Hamburg, she purchased first-class tickets for the train ride, which included sleeping berths. To our disappointment, we were forced to sit up all night in third class because we were Jews.

The compartment that we were riding in had a sign on the door that said JUDE, and a Star of David painted on it. This was to keep non-Jews out, as we were treated as a untermenschen or sub-human class of people.

We stood by the window and were able to roll it open. We talked to Paula and Anna until the train started to pull out of the station. Then we all started to cry. We realized we might never see each other again. We did not know what fate was in store for us.

Sitting up all night, we fell asleep by the motion of the train as it made its way to Hamburg. Soon it was morning and we arrived at our destination. The first leg of our journey was over.

We arrived in Hamburg on May 12. Since we could not ride the streetcar, we had to walk to the hotel, carrying our suitcases, where my mother hoped to rent lodging for one night. It was a long walk and we were tired when we arrived.

The manager remembered Max Freund, and helped us. During his travels, my father stayed there and established a good reputation. Under the Nazis, hotel guests had to register with the police. Even though it was dangerous for him and his staff, the manager did not list us as guests.

My mother took us for a meal at a harbor pub that she knew of. We returned to our room to rest and wait until it was time to board the MS St. Louis the next day, May 13, 1939.

In the morning, we left for the Hamburg American Lines dock to be cleared to board. Prior to embarking, the German customs agents checked our baggage to make sure we were obeying the law.

Everything was thrown around and we had to repack our belongings. Our money was counted. If they found too much money, or jewels in our suitcases, we would not be allowed to leave. We would be sent to a concentration camp where we would eventually perish. I saw a family being marched away because the agents found jewels hidden in their suitcase. We did not see them on the boat.

After the inspection of the luggage, the suitcases were stacked on skids and later delivered to the individual staterooms.

As we were early, we stood on the deck and watched other passengers board the ship. We watched the loading of fuel, food, water and baggage. It was horrible to look at many of the men. Their heads were shaven. They were still dirty since they had just been released from the concentration camp. They were allowed to leave because they had a ticket for the ship. They looked downcast and embarrassed. One could tell that they had been beaten.

Captain Gustav Schroeder had instructed the ships compliment, the crew, that we were to be treated as regular passengers, since we were on a cruise ship, even though we were unable to tip. As a result we were treated very well.

Once we boarded the ship, we entered a new world. It was a world of good food, friendly crewmembers, and serenity. People were sitting in chairs on the deck and waiters were passing around biscuits and consume from large trays. My family had retired to our stateroom to unpack. I was on deck to participate in the food. Having been on half rations, I was a very hungry boy.

Eventually I went to our first class cabin. I was told to take the top bunk. Liselotte was below me in the lower bunk. My mother and grandmother had single beds. We had a porthole and were able to watch the people on the dock.

It was bittersweet to leave Germany; I felt that from now on, life would be better for us. I was excited to be on a ship where I would have more freedom than ever before. Soon we would be in Havana, the first stop on our journey to the United States. I would miss our old home, but I knew we would be free in our new homeland.

I returned to the deck for our departure in the evening. As we left the dock, the band was playing "DO I HAVE TO LEAVE MY LITTLE VILLAGE?" Again I wondered if I would ever see Germany again. What was going to happen to me in the future? It was a fearsome thought. We were relieved to be out of the clutches of the Nazis.

People were in tears at the thought of never seeing their homeland again. We knew nothing about the language of our destination. We did not know English or Spanish. We were venturing into the unknown.

Everyone was excited and terrified. How would they make a living? How would they be received in Cuba and in the United States? How would they live? The professionals, the lawyers, doctors, and professors felt they would have to find new jobs and careers. They wondered whether or not they would be able to use the same skills they learned in Germany. First and foremost they would have to learn a new language.

My mother had no skills. She did not speak English. She did not know who would want to hire her.

We left with so little. Yet we left with a priceless gift: our lives.

On The High Seas

As SOON AS I COULD no longer see land I looked for my mother. She was not on the deck, so I went to our stateroom and found my mother, grandmother, and sister violently seasick.

Feeling very safe and free to be away from Germany and the strict rules that we were forced to follow, I wandered around the ship. Soon, I was tired and returned to our room.

Lulled to sleep by the rocking of the ship, I slept soundly that night. Arising early the next morning, my mother informed me that she and Grandma Ida were still too ill to take care of me, and I should find things to do. This was my first taste of freedom.

My mother told me not to go to the engine room. She heard that some of the crewmembers were Gestapo agents who were assigned to watch the Captain's crew.

Being hungry, I went to the dining deck. I could not read, therefore, the waiter read the menu to me. He cut my food for me. He was very kind to me. I was totally amazed at all the food. Since we were on half rations in Munich I was always hungry. Here, I ate like a king. I never tasted such delicious food and in such quantity.

Then I proceeded to explore the ship, heading first to the engine room. What an interesting sight it was. The smells of the machine oil and diesel fuel and clattering of the machinery were totally intriguing. No one bothered me or told me to leave.

There was a room next to the engine room that was empty when I was there. In later years I would learn the Gestapo agents met there. I was fortunate I was not there when they held their meeting.

I continued exploring the ship and looked into every nook and cranny. Eventually I returned to my stateroom to check in with my mother. I told her

I went to the engine room and nothing happened to me. She was too sick to react.

Checking on the daily posting of our position, I was surprised that we would pass by the Azores. I saw flying fish.

The trip to Cuba was restful and enjoyable for me. I felt completely safe. Consume was served every day on the deck. I went to the movies. There were children's activities I did not participate in because I did not know how. I watched the horse races on deck, which were games played by children. I wanted to go swimming, but did not have a bathing suit.

I had no social skills. I had no friends in Munich, so I played alone most of the time. But I had a good time standing on the sidelines watching the people socialize. I explored the ship by myself.

Every now and then, I would report in to my mother to tell her what was happening. They were always sick, so I was on my own the whole trip at sea. I would tell them what I was eating. I did not want them to think I was starving. This was not very nice of me, since they did not want to hear about food.

One day, a passenger, a retired professor, died of natural causes. He was devastated that he was forced to leave his beloved Germany and his life long colleagues. He was buried at sea that evening. The services were held on the port side. He was in a canvas bag, which was on a plank, and, ironically, a Nazi flag covered his remains.

At the conclusion of the service, the plank was tilted and his remains slid into the Atlantic Ocean. It promptly sank as weights were put into the bag. I was one of the spectators and was visibly shaken. It brought back thoughts of my father and I wondered about his funeral.

When we arrived in Havana Harbor, the first thing I noticed was the stifling heat and humidity. It was almost unbearable. I saw the white buildings along the waterfront. It was the fortress, El Moro, guarding the entrance to the harbor. This was most intriguing. Anything military held my interest.

We were getting ready to disembark. People were on deck already with their baggage. Then, we were told we could not depart the ship. Everything stopped. Tension mounted. It got worse when Cuban soldiers arrived and were stationed at strategic locations throughout the vessel. One soldier, a sergeant, took a liking to me and wanted to adopt me. We spent many moments together and he showed me his weapon and talked about his job. I wanted to go with him but my mother would not hear of it.

As we dropped anchor in the harbor, the ship was motionless and my mother and grandmother recovered from their seasickness. They came on deck to get fresh air and find out when we could leave the ship. Our bags were packed and we were ready. No news was relayed to the passengers. We waited and waited, and continued to wait.

Eventually, several families were able to leave which gave us hope that we would soon disembark. They had purchased legal entry visas into Cuba before they heard about the MS St. Louis. About thirty people left the ship, including one of the Gestapo agents.

One day, while looking down at the lighters, little Cuban boats that were gathering around the ship, my mother pointed to Uncle Werner. He flew down from New Jersey to see what he could do for us. He planned to help us get settled in Havana and also give us money for the essentials. He stayed for three days and then returned to his medical practice. I wanted to go with him and would have jumped off the ship, but my mother stopped me.

We finally realized we would not be able to disembark, because we had invalid visas. Mr. Gonzales sold us the visas and kept the money for himself.

Captain Schroeder took the ship to Miami, hoping that the United States would accept us, 907 Jews, fleeing for our lives. Not even the children were allowed to disembark.

At this time, June 5th, I had my eighth birthday, but we were too upset to even think about it. We had no time to think of a celebration. We were too distraught.

While languishing outside of Miami Beach, I noticed cars driving along the causeway. In a short time, a Coast Guard cutter approached us and ordered us to depart US territorial waters.

We returned to Havana, hoping the Cuban government would have a change of heart. We were allowed to get more food, water and fuel, but then we were forced to leave.

People were terrified. Some threatened to jump off the ship. One of the male passengers cut his right wrist and leaped overboard. The Cuban Harbor Police swiftly fished him out of the water and transported him to a Havana hospital. He later was transferred to a London mental institution where, in the 1960's he passed away.

Others wanted to commit mutiny, even though they did not know how to run a ship. Some considered suicide. The idea of returning to Germany was devastating, as we knew we would certainly be put in concentration camps and die.

The return trip to Europe proper was filled with trepidation, for we did not know where we would land. Captain Schroeder was determined to keep us safe. He would not return us to Germany.

A committee of some passengers was formed who kept the passengers in line, and informed. Captain Schroeder was a good man and let the group contact Mr. Troper, of the Joint Distribution Committee in the United States, who was trying to find a safe haven for us. Mr. Troper had raised money for us to go to the Dominican Republic, but President Roosevelt would not let that happen. He did not want us in the Western Hemisphere. When asked for entry into Canada, The Minister of Immigration commented: "None is one too many".

Mr. Troper was in touch with Belgium, which became the first country to voluntarily accept some passengers. Holland, England, and France shortly followed Belgiums lead. We were divided up as follows: 214 to Belgium, 181 to Holland, 288 to England, and 224 to France. My family was assigned to go to England, because we were a broken family without a man to look after us. We were happy to be off the European Continent.

When we were docked in Antwerp, Belgium, our first stop, a German freighter, the Rakotas, pulled up next to the MS St. Louis and we could see workers building bunks below the deck. Toilets were put on the deck. When it was finished, we walked on a plank from the MS St. Louis to the Rakotas. We never set foot in Belgium.

The ship had two holds, one for women and children, and the other, for males. I stayed with my family in the women's hold because I was only eight years old. It was a very uncomfortable trip, but we were not going to Germany.

We left for England, Monday, June 19,1939. We made a stop in Boulogne, France, on Tuesday to drop off the 224 passengers, and then left for Southampton, England. We arrived there on Wednesday, June 21, where we finally stepped on shore.

While under way, one of the passengers seemed to be annoying my mother, so I got in between him and my mother, and he grabbed me and threatened to throw me overboard. My mother stopped him and he stayed away from her for the rest of the trip to England.

All the passengers felt they were saved. Most were in for a shock, though, as September 1, 1939 turned our world upside down. It was the beginning of WWII.

We were aboard the MS St. Louis for forty days and forty nights.

Enemy Aliens

WE WERE HAPPY to go to England. In fact, most of the passengers wanted to go to England, since the English Channel would be a barrier to the Germans.

Upon disembarking the Rakotas at Southampton, we boarded a train for London. When we arrived in Victoria Station, the terminal was all decorated with red, white, and blue bunting, and flags. People were scurrying about, and I thought to myself that these people were so happy to see us. It turns out that the festivities were for visiting royalty. It brought some comfort and hope of stability to our formerly beleaguered existence.

The Jewish refugee group, who handled 288 of us, billeted the Freunds in, of all places, a brothel, much to my mothers chagrin, but it was really the first tranquil place we had for the last few years. My mother never told Grandma Ida what kind of hotel it was. I recall having squirrel for lunch. We informed Grandma Ida it was rabbit. She never knew the difference.

We had no money and were considered charity cases. The Joint Distribution Committee gave us money for essentials, food and toiletries.

Later, we were moved to a private home to live with a very nice English couple. The gentleman was a veteran of the British Army in WWI. He amassed a collection of books dealing with WWI. For hours I enjoyed looking at the pictures. I was frustrated because I could not read.

My mother noticed my frustration one rainy day, and purchased some basic reading books in order for me to learn how to read. That would have helped, but no one took the time to teach me. My mother, in her inability to teach me, used the books to teach herself a smattering of English.

We were free to travel anywhere in London. Our only constraint was lack of funds. We walked a lot, looked at the houses and stores and missed our neighborhood in Munich.

One day we came upon a black gentleman, on a street corner. As I never saw anyone of that race, I was totally enthralled, and asked my mother numerous questions, some rather intimate. I wanted to know how he lived, since someone had read LITTLE BLACK SAMBO to me. I asked my mother what he ate, and she replied, "regular food as we do".

On September 1, 1939, WWII broke out. We were issued gas masks and assigned to an air raid shelter. There was one dug in the park near our residence. I watched the barrage balloons, which were large balloons connected to each other with nets, and tethered to the ground, rise into the sky to protect the buildings from being strafed by the German planes. The "ack ack" gunners would practice anti-aircraft traversing. They moved the guns up, down, and sideways.

It was not long thereafter when we were told that as enemy aliens we would be relocated outside of London. My mother told them that we did not care about Germany and were not the enemy. This did not matter.

We were settled in Yelverton, north of Plymouth. This was a village in Southern England, serviced by a local steam engine. It was a Victorian village with quaint houses clustered around a large communal square. It was on the edge of the Dartmoor Moor. Wild horses ran in the neighborhood. One day Liselotte got too close to a horse and was kicked. She was not hurt, but from then on, was afraid of horses.

We were quartered in a small pension, just on the edge of the square. We were assigned a very small room with a pot bellied stove and communal bathroom. In Munich we lived in a large residence, which also had enough room for our servants. I imagined it must have been rather difficult for my mother and Grandma Ida to have been reduced to an almost beggar like existence.

We took long walks in the Dartmoor Moor, gathering blueberries for supper. We were fed one meal each day at the bed and breakfast where we stayed. As we were restricted to the area, we did not see much of Plymouth. I did go to the dentist in Plymouth for a toothache.

I was fortunate enough to be allowed to attend a small private school for some of the St. Louis children. There, I learned to speak some English. Best of all we could hear military music and we would spend most of our time marching around the classroom, thus not learning much English.

In December, 1939, we were summoned to London in preparation for our departure to our long sought after goal, the United States of America. We were very eager to join our family in Hackensack, New Jersey.

By this time I had out grown most of the clothes that we brought from Munich. No other clothes were provided for me, so I wore clothes that were too small, and very uncomfortable.

While in London, we were given more freedom of movement, and extra money, so we were able to do some sight seeing. We also went to the movies, and ate fish and chips wrapped in newspaper purchased from a street vender. What a good meal it was.

Before we could leave, we had to report to the US Embassy for a final check on our mental stability, physical health, and to insure positive identification.

We were in England six months before our quota number came up to immigrate to the United States.

We departed from Southampton on the Swedish ship, the Stockholm. The trip must have been rather dull, as I have no recollection of what occurred on the ship except that at night it was ablaze so the German U boats knew we were a neutral vessel and not to harm us.

In 1956, the Stockholm collided with another passenger ship, the Andréa Dora, which sank off the coast of Cape Cod. The Stockholm returned to Sweden.

Ida with twins Thea and Edith   Thea and Edith

Lauchheimer twins (Thea & Edith), Max Freund

Siegfried Lauchheimer   Cantor Hohenemser
grandfather d 1925

Thea and Phil (at age 2) with Paula the Governess

Phil in Munich

Max Joseph Freund, father

Rendering of Max Joseph Freund

LT Max J. Freund
WWI, 5th Inf Rg, German Army

Phil with mother Thea

Phil, with Thea, Margarette,
and grandmother Ida

Ida Lauchheimer, grandmother

Phil graduates G. Washington HS,
NYC June 1950

Mother Thea, Grandmother
Ida, Aunt Edith Gould

Ellwangen parade, rear seat – Burgermeister,
LTC H.D.Weston, CO 103 Eng Bn, 28 Inf Div,
front seat CPL Phil Freund, driver

PVT P Freund Basic Training,
Camp Atterbury IN 1951

COL P.S. Freund, MI ,Hqs Intel & Security
Cmnd, Washington DC, 1975 - 1991

COL Phil Freund, Mark Freund

Thea Herz nee Freund,
nee Lauchheimer

30

Belle Anne and Phil
Married in 1957

Our children (from left to right), Mark,
Jacqueline, Margarette and Perry.

Belle Anne and Phil
Munich, Germany — 2007

Sen H. Kohl and Phil,
presentation of Proclamation. 2009

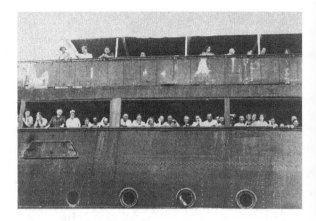

MS St. Louis – Captain Gustav Schröder, the commander of the ship, was a non-Jewish German and an anti-Nazi who went to great lengths to ensure dignified treatment for his passengers. He arranged for Jewish religious services and commanded his crew to treat the refugee passengers as they would any other customers of the cruise line. As the situation of the vessel deteriorated, he personally negotiated and schemed to find them a safe haven (for instance, at one point he formulated plans to wreck the ship on the British coast to force the passengers to be taken as refugees). He refused to return the ship to Germany until all the passengers had been given entry to some other country. He was eventually honored in Israel and Germany following WWII.

Passengers on board the MS St. Louis

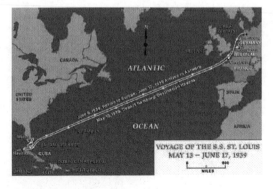

Voyage of the MS st. Louis
May 13 - June 17, 1939

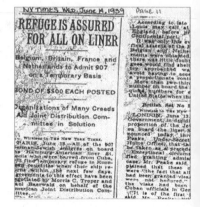

NY Times news article

Concerned relatives who came to be of assistance, in Havana Harbour. Uncle Werner was in one of the small lighters (boats).

A view of the MS St. Louis surrounded by smaller vessels in the port of Havana

Telegram appealing unsuccessfully to FDR to help.

Phil, in center, with other children on board the MS S. Louis

Early Life In America

CHRISTMAS EVE, 1939, we landed in Weehawken, New Jersey. Uncle Werner was there to greet us. He took us to his home in Hackensack, where Santa Claus, Sam Reich, a doctor in Hackensack who was Uncle Werner's friend, was there to greet us. Aunt Edith and Cousin Arthur were also waiting for us.

As we were celebrating our safe arrival, I heard, in the distance, a train whistle. Thinking that America was about to experience an air raid, I dove under a table, much to the hilarity of one and all.

We stayed with Aunt Edith and Uncle Werner in Hackensack for a few months. My mother sold chocolate from door to door as a distributor for a chocolate company. A few months later she found a job in New York, in the garment industry, sewing collars on t-shirts, for $.25 an hour. This was the first of several sewing jobs. It was decided, rather than travel so far to New York, my mother, Grandma Ida, and Lisa, would move to New York.

My mother, Grandma, and sister moved to an apartment in Washington Heights, Manhattan. It was a cold-water tenement. The apartment was located on the fourth floor, and with no elevator. To use hot water, one put a nickel in the meter, which was located inside by the apartment door.

The garbage was sent down to the basement on the dumb waiter, using a rope to control the movement. The janitor would remove the garbage and we would pull the dumb waiter back up to our apartment.

Grandma Ida had her own bedroom, and my mother and sister shared a bedroom. In the large living room was a couch that I slept on when visiting, and later when I moved in.

Since my mother could not afford to raise me, I stayed in Hackensack, in order to have a father image from Uncle Werner, and to be a companion to Arthur. Arthur and I liked being together and got along very well. Aunt Edith was like a mother to me. Many times I called her mother, since she looked just like my mother, as they were identical twins. Living there was very nice for me.

My mother worked in a factory where the workers were locked in during the day. They had bathroom privileges twice a day, once in the morning and once in the afternoon. Eventually, she became one of the leaders that brought in the Union and better working conditions. She was well liked and the workers listened to her.

Grandma Ida found a job working for a contractor who made military ribbons that were awards and decorations. Military personal wore these ribbons on their uniforms.

In January, 1940, my mother enrolled me in State Street School in Hackensack. Because I could not read or write any language, I started school in the second grade, rather than the third. George Coty was assigned to be my mentor. He took good care of me in school as well as out. He took me to the library to get a library card, which was important for me to have. This would allow me to borrow books.

We walked up the steps to the library and I was very impressed with this old building. We went to the librarian, who was sitting at a large wooden mahogany desk.

George said, "Philip needs a library card".

"But I am Jewish," I said.

"That does not matter." the librarian said.

"But I have no money."

"You do not need money. What is your name?"

"Philip Freund."

"Where do you live?"

"219 Passaic Street."

"Oh, you are one of Doc Gould's boys."

"Yes."

She filled out the paper work and said,

"Here is your card."

I was indoctrinated into believing that Jews did not have the same rights as others.

George told me I could take any book home as long as I returned it when it was due. I thought "what a country." I picked a book about cave men. I don't know why. Eventually, I would read the whole series. I was determined to be the best American that I could be and that meant reading, reading, and more reading. I wanted the United States to be glad we were here.

I was determined to be more American than the Americans and to make a contribution to the betterment of this country.

The refusal for us to land in Cuba had a great effect on us. We thought no one wanted any part of us. When we were refused entry into the United States, it felt as if we were not worthwhile. This affected me for the rest of my life and I continue to feel that I have to prove myself worthy to live in this magnificent country.

By the time I was in the fifth grade, I was reading at the 10th grade level. Reading and the radio were my escape. When I was not reading, Arthur and I would listen to programs like "Captain Midnight", "Mandrake the Magician" and "The Green Hornet".

I played baseball in public school. Since I wanted to be accepted by my teammates, I did most everything they did. With one exception: One day they chewed tobacco behind the school. They got really sick. I pretended I was chewing, but chewed black licorice instead and spit out the black juice. I did not get sick, but nobody noticed.

When the United States entered the war in 1941, Uncle Werner volunteered his services as a doctor in the US Army Medical Corps. He went to Carlisle Barracks, Pennsylvania, for basic training. From 1942-1943, he was stationed in California. From there, he was sent to Adak Islands in the Aleutians, where he spent one year. Being a dermatologist, he was needed to treat tropical skin diseases.

He was later assigned to a hospital in Richmond, VA, until 1945 when he was discharged.

Uncle Werner's mother, Jenny Gould, left Germany in 1939, and went to Lisbon, Portugal where she stayed until her quota number came up. She arrived in New Jersey in 1941, months before my uncle left for his tour of duty. She and Aunt Edith were in charge of three boys, me and cousins

Arthur, and Steven, who was born shortly before Uncle Werner left for the war zone.

Grandma Jenny cooked and helped take care of us. She and Aunt Edith were often at odds as to who was in charge of the household. They had a very strained relationship. Grandma Jenny was very good to me and I loved her very much. She was not my real grandmother but she treated me like I was her grandson.

Grandma Jenny hoarded candy and she would share it mostly with me. She let me help her grate potatoes for dumplings, until I scraped my fingers and they started bleeding. She let me pick up the Saturday Evening Post, Americas oldest magazine, with a dime she gave me every week. I felt important to her.

During the weekends from September to May, Arthur and I had a lot of freedom. Arthur rode the bus all day long and got to know all the schedules. I stayed home because I had no money to ride the bus. I liked to help Grandma Jenny and Aunt Edith. Most of the time we made fake flowers, which a vendor sold. I read in my spare time.

Sometimes Arthur and I took care of Steven. We took him for buggy rides. We rolled him and our dog down the hill. He laughed when he fell out of the buggy. I played ball with him when he was old enough to hold a ball. He loved being with us.

Aunt Edith took in two boarders to help pay the bills. Their names were Lt and Mrs. Johnson, and were very kind to all of us. He was an Army Military Police Officer, who was assigned to the Port of Embarkation in Brooklyn, New York. He rode the bus and subway to work and back everyday. It was great to have an adult male in the house. Many years later he and I met in Vienna, Austria, when I was stationed with the 796th MP Battalion, the only multi-national peace keeping force in Europe.

One Saturday, Arthur and I were playing in Uncle Werner's car that was on blocks in the garage. We rocked the car so much that it fell off the blocks. The filling station owner was George. His gas station was close to our house. I visited him occasionally, after school. He let me pick up the garbage and help him wash cars, and he paid me with a few pennies. George was our friend and helped us with the car. He put the car back on the blocks. No one found out what we had done, as there was no damage to the car.

Arthur and I built a wagon out of an old buggy that we found. We used pieces of wood for the sides. We used the wagon when we went to the dump to collect soda and milk bottles to sell to the local grocery store for 2 cents a soda bottle and 8 cents a milk bottle. We collected enough bottles to go to the movies, buy candy for 2 cents, and buy several comic books for 5 cents each.

Uncle Werner decided, as I got older, I must be groomed to take care of my mother. He found summer jobs for me, before he went into the Army. He was gone for three years, only coming home for a month each year. When I was eleven years old, I was sent to a chicken farm to work for my room and board and help the farmer. I would spend three summers on this farm.

I do not recall seeing my family during the summer. While Aunt Edith, Grandma Jenny and Arthur and later Steve spent time at a rented home on the beach, in Belmar, New Jersey all summer, I picked up the dead chickens every morning from the coops. I tried not to be attacked by the live roosters, who were very aggressive, and territorial. I threw the dead chickens in a pit and burned them.

I fed the chickens and gave them water. We butchered chickens for dinner every day. For years I could not eat chicken. When I joined the army, I regained my taste for deep fried chicken.

The second summer, in the evenings, I helped to hunt for rats which attacked the chickens after the rats got in the coops. We used a two by four with nails driven into the wood. We tried to hit them with our homemade weapon. During the day, I kept busy with odd jobs the farmer assigned me. I raked apples in the orchard and swept out the barn.

One evening, when it was very dark, I thought I saw one of the cats living on the farm. I bent down to pet it. It turned out to be a skunk. I was on the receiving end of the skunks spray. I got undressed outside, and was hosed down with water. The farmers' wife washed me with lye soap to get rid of the smell. My clothes were washed in tomato juice. That ended my rat hunting.

Other boys came to this farm for a recreational vacation. They would stay for one or two weeks. During the day, they played at the farm or went to town, Franklin, to shop or go to the movies. They were nice to me but we all understood our place. They were on vacation and I was there to work. Some evenings, I played ball with them, if I did not have a job to do.

When I was thirteen, I was strong enough to have a job requiring muscle. I shoveled chicken manure into a large wagon. The manure was taken into a field to be used for the crops.

There was a large combine, which harvested the grain. I tied a bag onto the machine and when the bag was full, I would secure the bag, remove it and tie on another bag, tossing the first bag off of the combine. I worked fast to keep up with the bags.

I ate well and I did not miss my family. The owners of the farm were like parents to me and showed me a lot of love.

I grew fond of a pig, and he of me, and he became my pet. This was short lived, as one day I was made to watch my friend be butchered for a meal. I cried for days at the loss of my pig. This was one of life's hard lessons.

The money I made, about $0.25 a week, was given to my mother to help pay for the household expenses. I was always glad to go back to school in the fall.

After Uncle Werner returned home in 1945. He looked for a summer home to purchase and in 1946 he found one at Upper Greenwood Lake, New Jersey. I learned how to swim by jumping into the water and being told to swim or drown. Uncle Werner gave me ten minutes of instruction and rowed out into the lake. He told me to jump in. I swam. The day came when I swam from one side of the lake to the other.

Eventually, when I was fourteen years old, Uncle Werner found jobs for me, for the summer, in Hackensack. I would stay with him during the week while the rest of the family went to the lake. Uncle Werner and I went to the lake each weekend. Sometimes mother and Lisa joined us. All day Saturday and every Sunday morning, I removed garbage for the "Upper Greenwood Lake Association". While the rest of the family enjoyed the fun, I was working. I came home at night and jumped into the lake to get rid of the horrible odor. Again, my money went to help my mother.

On Sunday afternoons, I participated in motor boat races on the lake. Uncle Werner had the boat built out of plywood at Upper Greenwood Lake. Arthur was not allowed to take part, because it was too dangerous for him to race a boat. I was allowed and I really enjoyed the thrill of racing.

New York

GRANDMA IDA INSISTED that I learn to read and write German. I hated Germany for forcing us to leave and did not want to have anything to do with the language. I wanted to be totally American. I had no choice in the matter.

While living in New Jersey, during the school year, I visited the family in New York every weekend when I was twelve and a half. Since I did not have bus fare, I walked from Hackensack to Manhattan, about seven miles, every Saturday and back every Sunday. I walked across the George Washington Bridge alone on the pedestrian path.

Grandma Ida worked with me at the kitchen table the minute I walked in the door. She had the Aufbau, a Reconstruction German Jewish newspaper, ready for me to read the articles out loud in German to her. I would then write a paragraph about what I had read, in German. We conversed in German. I became very fluent which helped me when I joined the army.

Grandma Jenny and Grandma Ida were very good to me. I liked to do them favors and they appreciated the fact I did not fight with them. I think they felt pity for me. I was not treated the same as my cousins. Arthur and Steve, were not expected to do much. In the summer, I did the yard work, and in the winter I shoveled the snow by myself.

When I was approaching the age of thirteen, I attended Hebrew classes in New York. On Saturday afternoons I prepared for my Bar Mitzvah. I went to Rabbi Baerwald's house, our friend and Rabbi from Munich. He patiently taught me the Hebrew prayers.

My ceremony was very simple. There was no big party, just the immediate family. Uncle Werner was home on leave from the military and attended with Aunt Edith, my mother, grandmother and sister. I was proud of my achievement, and received a few books, which I loved.

When I turned fifteen and entered High School, I moved to New York, and was enrolled at George Washington High School. My bedroom was the living room couch. My clothes were kept in the broom closet.

I attended school during the day, and worked at whatever job I could find during the evening hours and weekends. The money helped make life easier for my mother, Grandmother, and sister. Uncle Werner always found used clothing for me. My shoes were left overs from the shoe cobbler. One pair was so small that I started having foot problems.

My mother rode the subway to work and back. Once in a while, when I was not working and it was raining out, I took an umbrella and met her at the subway station. This was when she vented to me about her life.

I felt bad, but I could not do anything to console her and help her change her attitude. She felt like she was at a dead end, living with her mother forever. The three females, including my sister, were always fighting.

I was glad to leave the house and go to work. I joined after school sports. I became part of the track team and ran my lungs out every day. I was on the swimming team. I bonded with my teammates. I was in charge of the High School Hall Patrol Service Squad, which monitored the doors and cleaned up the corridors. This was my own special therapy.

Next to my mothers apartment lived Erik Hagen. He was a refugee from Berlin where he worked as a newspaper editor. In New York, he worked in the hotel industry hanging curtains in the hotel rooms. Some Sunday mornings he took me for walks around Washington Heights, in New York City, we talked about politics, religion, and reincarnation. I really enjoyed his company.

During the summers, in New York, I was employed at a different job each year. I worked for an auto dealership, undercoating cars. I was a janitor in a ladies undergarment factory. I worked in a rock quarry. I was a stevedore. If I was lucky, I spent a weekend at the summer home. My family went there many weekends. The Gould family spent most of the summer at the summer home. I was expected to help pay for the families expenses, and was not allowed to keep any of my earnings.

My uncle did not think I was too smart and told me many times that I should plan on working in a factory when I graduated high school. My grades were not good, but that was because I was allowed very little time to study. I was working long hours.

I needed to pass the "Regent Board Exams" to graduate and surprisingly, I passed with a good score. This was encouraging to me.

On June 25, 1950, I graduated High School. It was the day the Korean War started.

During the summer of 1950, I worked as a lifeguard and camp counselor at a summer resort in Bushkill Falls, Pennsylvania. I saved some money to start college in the fall.

Artistic Foundations

IN SEPTEMBER, 1950, I started working at Artistic Foundations, delivering mail within the company. Later, I was trained to work on a multilith 1250, a high-speed mimeograph machine. Being colorblind, I had to constantly consult with others as to what colors to use.

This was a Jewish firm, which owned knitting mills in Manchester, New Hampshire. I worked in the headquarters at 417 5th Ave., in New York City. My co-workers were very good to me and helped me with my job.

One of the men told me he was in the Battle of the Bulge, part of the 110th Infantry Regiment, 28th Infantry Division. He lived to tell about it. I was very impressed. A few months later, I returned for a visit before going to Germany with the Army. I wanted to tell this man I was now part of the103rd Engineering Battalion of the 28th Infantry Division.

Because Mr. Levine, my boss, knew I was poor, he scheduled me for a lot of over time, including Saturdays when I earned time and a half an hour, $1.50. This was a godsend. I was able to buy a little TV for my family.

Grandma loved to watch wrestling and we sat together and she laughed during the whole program. It made me feel good that I brought her some joy.

We also watched the Milton Berle Hour, which was very funny. The announcer was Sid Stone, who was a pharmacist at the drug store where I was the errand boy on weekends.

Riding the subway to work was terrible for me. It was crowded, it smelled bad, and people were rude.

Night school started in September at New York University in Greenwich Village, and I signed up for three classes, Geology, English and History. I had a strong desire to attend college. I went three nights a week and traveled on the subway.

There was no time for me to go home for supper so I would go to the Horn & Hardart Automat on 33rd Street and Broadway. There, I made a soup of hot water and catsup in a cup. The crackers were free, and I would fill up on them.

Once in a while, on my way to school, I stopped to see Madie and Werner Blank who had settled in New York. They always had some clothing for me as well as a hot meal. They were good to me and helped me when I needed it.

I successfully passed these courses, but NYU was extremely expensive. I was working, and attending school, and my social life suffered. There was no time for friends or even going to the movies.

The next semester, I enrolled at City College of New York, which was free. I took a bookkeeping class. The class was not very difficult for me, but the time came for me to move on. I dropped out of school in the middle of the semester.

On March 15, 1951, during my lunch hour, I went to Time Square, to the recruiting station, and told the recruiter that I wanted to enlist. He was happy to see me. I told him that I would be back on the 19th since I had to first celebrate my Grandmother Ida's birthday.

My home situation was bad. I was tired of sleeping on the couch. I was tired of the women screaming at each other. I was tired of the subway.

The apartment smelled bad and I did not like where we were living.

Uncle Werner had strongly suggested that I join the Army.

When the Korean War started, Uncle Werner again suggested I join the Army. I would be lucky to retire as a sergeant in twenty years. Most of the money would have to be sent home to my mother. Out of $75, I sent $25 to her each month, for the next three years, even after she married and moved to Wisconsin.

Basic Training and
Advanced Individual Training

MY PAPER WORK, IEF (Initial Enlistment Forms), was completed on March 15, and I was sworn into the Army on March 19, 1951, in New York City at the Whitehall Induction Center on Whitehall Street.

My mother rode the subway with me to her work stop, on March 19. I would catch the bus at this stop. We said our good-byes and I went on to the recruiting station with my little bag of toiletries. I remember my mother crying as she walked away. She did not know when she would see me again.

When I left New York, I was with a busload of about thirty recruits. We arrived at Fort Devens, Massachusetts, and were assigned to our bunks. Oh, what a surprise when we debussed. It was already late at night and the NCOs, non-commissioned officers, seemed to be in some sort of rage as they screamed, cursed, and tried to make us as miserable as possible. We were assigned to a dilapidated wooden building, which seemed to have been built around WWI.

After a few hours of sleep, we were awakened at 4:00AM to more verbal abuse, and told to hurry up. After completing our morning constitution, we were herded into a huge dining facility, AKA, also known as, the mess hall. We were handed metal trays with cutouts. As we walked through the cafeteria line, the mess attendants "plopped" food into the cutouts.

We were then herded to picnic tables, and were told to hurry and eat before our ten minutes were up. I took a cup of coffee, and inserted two level teaspoons full of sugar. At least, I thought it was sugar. It turned out to be salt. At that moment, all I could think of was that "this Army makes terrible coffee".

As we were about to leave, I saw in front of me an NCO not allowing anyone to throw away uneaten, undesirable, portions. I quickly stuffed my face to avoid his wrath.

Once outside, we were taught how to get into formation. We were taught military courtesy and then were led to get our clothing. Oh what joy. New clothes. I could hardly contain myself with happiness.

One of the quartermaster clerks measured everyone's feet. I was informed that I would be a size 9.5, and for years this was my size, until many years later when I found out that I was a size ten.

We were sent back to the barracks and ordered to put on our new uniforms. Everything was too big on us. We looked like a bunch of rag muffins. What a sight. All these new soldiers were in their HBT's, fatigues-herring bone twill. We went to get our picture taken. We looked like a bunch of sad sacks.

Soon it was lunchtime. We were fed a meal that I can still recall how good it was. Meat, gravy, potatoes, vegetables, dessert and coffee.

We started in-processing that afternoon. We were put into a large building with tables and chairs, and were given the AFQT, Armed Forces Qualification Test. I already took the ASVAB, aptitude-armed services vocational aptitude battery tests, but not the foreign language fluency test. I was tested in speaking, reading, and writing German. These tests took a day and a half. I passed with flying colors, thanks to Grandma Ida.

I was given a physical and waited at camp, while all the others were shipped to Camp Pickett, Virginia, to the 43rd Infantry Division. Being alone in the barracks until new recruits came the next day, I was able to get some well-needed sleep.

On Easter Sunday, I was awakened and told to report to the mess sergeant in the mess hall as a KP, kitchen police. As I walked to the mess hall, I was joined by other KP's reporting to the same destination. One of the KP's mentioned if you are late, you get assigned to the grease pit.

I hurried to the mess hall and entered the first door I saw. When inside, we were lined up and the mess sergeant calling names. As he did not call my name, I decided to leave. Just then, I heard the sergeant yell at me "where the hell do you think you are going?". In a meek voice I answered, as my name was not called, I was going back to bed. He, in turn, roared with laughter and told me to get my ass to the other side and report to the sergeant in charge of the grease pit.

When I arrived at the other side of the building, I told the sergeant who I was and he told me to take off my jacket and under shirt, as this was a filthy job. The grease trap is a metal box under the sink, which collects the grease. Then the grease is pumped out to a truck. My job was to unscrew the top and reach down into the trap, which was about 18 inches high and about 18 inches wide. I had to release a valve to allow the grease to flow into the truck and thoroughly scrub the inside of the trap. As I opened the top, the stench was over powering and I immediately threw up. The mess sergeant screamed a long list of obscenities to include "you damn civilians, you always throw up".

Afterwards, I proceeded to scrub out the grease trap. I was covered with grease from fingertips to shoulders. There was grease on my chest, face, and hair. My pants were covered with grease. What a mess. I replaced the cover and when the sergeant was not looking, I sneaked out the door and headed back to the barracks. I went to take a shower.

After showering, I washed my uniform in the deep sink. The sergeant from the kitchen came looking for "that no good KP". He inquired as to where the sick soldier was. I informed him some smelly kid took off and went to the infirmary. He did not recognize me, since I was not wearing clothes and did not have my glasses on. He left, and I dressed and went to the Service Club, where I spent the rest of the day. I went to a different mess hall for dinner.

I received orders to report to Camp Atterbury, Indiana, to the 28th Infantry Division, 103rd Engineers. After the new recruits were in-processed, I boarded a train with them and traveled to Indiana. It was my first visit to the Mid-West. The friends I made on the train were assigned to the 628th Medium Tank Battalion. I was assigned to the 103rd Combat Engineers Battalion. I completed three years of math in High School and was considered proficient to be a combat engineer. Sadly, I never saw these friends again.

Basic training was no picnic. Since I was on the track team in High School, I was in good physical shape. We did a lot of running which was no hardship for me, but hard for other soldiers, not in shape.

A combat engineer is first and foremost an infantry soldier and is trained to fight with a rifle and bayonet. He also receives training in such interesting fields as mine laying, mine removal, flame throwing, explosives, bridge building, booby traps, construction, road maintenance, demolitions, and operating heavy equipment. I loved it.

Camp Atterbury was a remnant of WWII. All the barracks were made of wood. Soft coal permeated the air and stunk like sulfur. I was assigned to A Company and lived in the barracks with 139 other soldiers. Needless to say, it was very crowded. There was a measles epidemic. I contacted the disease and spent a week in the hospital.

I returned to A Company Basic Platoon 1, with Lt Bob Vernon, my platoon leader. Lt Vernon was a tall and very strong officer. He was an excellent example of what a combat engineer should be. One of the basic assignments of a combat engineer is to build bridges anywhere, from large floating bridges, to small bridges, to infantry assault bridges.

An infantry Assault Bridge floats on little boats called pontoons, and placed crossways over the pontoons is a duck walk with a rope guardrail running on both sides of the duck walk.

I was trained to build an Assault Bridge. My assignment was to bring the struts, which held the handrail rope to the duck walk.

The worst part was building bridges where we spent a whole week in water up to our armpits. I was going to grow webbing between my toes.

The river was moving very rapidly from the melting snow up stream. I could see the men building the bridge were going to need more struts, so I grabbed several of them and started across the bridge. As I was about one fourth of the way across, it lurched, throwing me over the side. I must have hit my head on one of the pontoons. I was unconscious as I went under the bridge, and floated down stream face down.

Lt Vernon saw what happened and immediately dove into the water and rescued me. When I was conscious, I was informed that Lt Vernon saved my life. I thanked him, but he shrugged it off and said, "It was all in the line of duty". The last time I saw Lt Vernon was in Germany at a unit picnic baseball game. I heard that he lost a son in Vietnam and he has since passed away.

One of the saddest events during basic training was the loss of one of our troopers, Private Mizrachi. We were building a Bailey Bridge and he decided to goof off. The bridge was being built over a bluff and he went under the bridge at the bottom of the bluff, to catch a nap, as we did not get much sleep during basic training.

The Bailey Bridge is built like an erector set in pieces and is pushed across, over the water, until it reaches the other side. One segment fell and tragically crushed Private Mizrachi. Three of us were sent down to see if he was still alive and, if possible, extract him from the wreckage. I found him with a beam running parallel on his body.

One day I was assigned KP and my specific job was to wash the windows. As I am washing the windows, I thought, "I could do this for twenty years". I thought about my future and at that point I decided that being a soldier for twenty years would not be bad. I would get medical coverage, and a pension. Once I became a veteran, I would have the GI bill for my education and the VA for medical coverage, life insurance, and prescription drug coverage. At that point, I made a decision to stay in the military in some shape or form.

After Basic Training, I went to AIT, which is Advanced Individual Training. I was asked to become a radio operator and spent half a morning listening to Morse Code – ditty da da. I knew this would drive me crazy, so I quit.

Since I enlisted into the regular army, I could choose what job I wanted. I was offered the job of explosives specialist and decided to try that assignment, as I was assigned to the 103rd Engineers due to my math knowledge which would be useful to determine explosive amounts. I spent one week learning about the different explosives, such as ammonium nitrate, shaped charges, bangalor torpedoes, primer cord and C3. Graduation consisted of making a tank trap. I was the last one to be tested.

Lt Gay was the OIC, Officer in Charge. He told me to take the jeep and get more explosives. I went to the demolition bunker and saw there were six canisters of ammonium nitrate. I put them in the jeep trailer to take out to the testing area. I dug six holes, approximately ten feet apart, into which I put the six canisters, and told Lt Gay I was prepared to explode them.

After giving me the go-ahead signal, I cranked the charging unit, yelled "fire in the hole" three times, and exploded 300 pounds of ammonium nitrate. The sky was filled with dirt, rocks, and even a tree. The hole was big enough to put a small house in it. Lt Gay asked me how much of the explosives I used. When I told him six canisters, each weighing 50 pounds, he was not happy. I was not supposed to use all of it, as that was all he had. I wonder if the hole is still there.

In July, 1951, a call went out for volunteers to go to Fort Bragg, North Carolina, to become paratroopers. The inducement was an extra $50 a month. I figured the extra money, added to my base pay of $75, would make me rich. I was selected, even though I wore glasses, because I could run with boots on.

I arrived at Fayetteville, North Carolina, after a long train ride. I was amazed to find there were two kinds of water fountains, and two kinds of bathrooms, one for whites and one for blacks.

When the bus for Fort Bragg came, I stepped aboard with all my gear. The only empty seat was at the rear of the bus. Having lived in New Jersey and New York, I was used to riding with black people. The driver yelled at me to go to the front of the bus. I told him that there were no seats. I was carrying my duffle bag and my backpack. He refused to move the bus until I went to the front. One of the other passengers said to me "please soldier, go to the front of the bus so that we can go home".

When I arrived at Fort Bragg, I reported to the orderly room. I was assigned to a bunk, a wall locker, and a footlocker, and became part of the 82nd Airborne Division. I made up my bed, went to dinner and then to sleep.

The next morning, we were rousted out of bed by a sergeant/instructor. We barely had enough time to use the latrine before we were hustled out on the street for roll call.

We went on a run everyday. It felt good to be physically active. As we ran we greeted everyone with "airborne all the way". This was accomplished wearing boots, long fatigue pants, a t-shirt and head covering. When we returned to the barracks we made our beds, and went for breakfast.

The second week, we were introduced to the 35-foot tower. We put on a parachute harness attached to a cable, which ran from the top of the tower to the ground. Close to the end was a sand pit. We were to hook up to the cable, jump off the tower, and land correctly in the sand pit.

A soldier, in front of me, jumped out. Some of the lines got wrapped around his throat and he gurgled all the way down. Then, I decided this was not worth an extra $50 a month, so I told the jumpmaster I quit. He told me to walk down. As I walked down, I realized I washed out. I walked to the barracks and packed my things. I returned to the 103rd ENGR as a paratrooper failure.

Arriving in the orderly room, I was told to report back to the 103rd Engineers, which by this time were involved with a maneuver on post called "Operation Southern Pines". We were supposedly engaged in mortal combat against the 43rd Division. I reported to Battalion Headquarters and was assigned to the recon section which was part of the Intelligence, S2, Section. I attained the rank of PFC and was assigned my own jeep, trailer, and chance for the next promotion. What a deal.

One day I was sauntering down a dusty road and came across some 43rd Division soldiers guarding a crossing. I thought to myself,"wouldn't it be nice if I captured these guys". I leveled my rifle at them and told them to surrender. They laughed at me and told me to take off, before they beat the crap out of me.

One of them asked me where I was from. When I replied, Milwaukee, he said "me too". We started a friendship lasting until he passed away in 1992. He was a star athlete and an excellent math teacher. Peter Cucinello and I taught together in Oak Creek, WI and for the Milwaukee Public Schools until we retired in 1990.

After looking all over for my group, I finally found them in the field with help from a jeep driver who knew where they were and took me to their location. They were all glad to see me when I came back. The next day they were asked to build a floating bridge and since I was in the S2 section I did not participate.

One day I was told to turn in my dirty clothes, as there was a field laundry down the road. I decided I should walk to the field laundry myself because I wanted my own clothes back. If I put them in the big pile I might never see them again. As I walked down the road I crossed the river where they were building the bridge. On the opposite side of the bridge abutment, I saw a POL, Petroleum Oil and Lubricant, unit. I told them of my plight. It was 103 degrees out. I needed to take a shower and wash my clothes.

One soldier said to me he could not help with the shower, but could give me a large container of gasoline, which I could use to wash my clothes. I did. Afterwards one of the guys told me I should not get too close to any fires or I would be torched. I reeked of gasoline for three weeks. It was so bad that one day somebody dropped off a bunch of clothes for me just so I would not smell, but I did anyway.

While at Operation Southern Pines we were warned to be careful when getting into our pup tents. We were told to shake out our sleeping bags and check our boots, as snakes liked to crawl into those two things. I heard that a soldier in another unit was bitten.

At the conclusion of Operation Southern Pines, we traveled by train back to Camp Atterbury. It was my first experience sleeping in a Pullman car. A freight car was attached to the train in which our meals were cooked. We ate out of our mess kits and there was a large garbage can with an immersion heater filled with water so we could wash our mess kits. The problem was when the train lurched, water splashed out and we would get wet.

We arrived back at Camp Atterbury and were informed that we would be going to either Germany or Korea. I was ordered, as were 50% of the Engineers, to go to Korea. I felt I could be of greater service to the army utilizing my German language skills. I spoke to Lt George Arnold from Connecticut. "I could serve the army better as a linguist". His answer was "find a unit that will take you to Germany and I will release you".

I walked around Camp Atterbury. Near the headquarters of the 28th Division, by chance, I asked another soldier coming from the opposite direction if he knew of a unit going to Germany. He said "yes", and he pointed to a one-story building, which had a sign that said 28 CIC, Counter Intelligence Company.

I entered the building, and asked who was in charge. Someone pointed to one of the men, who was wearing a t-shirt, bloused pants and boots. He was also smoking a cigar. I approached him and asked if he was in need of a German linguist. He looked at me questioningly and said "Yes. Are you a certified, qualified, linguist?" I answered yes. He then wanted to know what unit I was assigned to and informed me he would check up on what I had told him and if it was true, he would personally request a transfer for me.

Upon returning to the barracks I started packing. I rolled up my mattress, folded my sheets and pillowcase, and turned everything into the supply room. Everyone was under the impression I was getting ready to go to Korea. I went back to the barracks, sat on my bed and waited. Somehow I knew someone would be coming for me shortly.

It was around dinner when a member of the 28th CIC unit came in looking for me. He took me to the building where I had been previously. I was assigned to a barracks and I drew my bedding from the supply room. I went to the mess hall for supper, went back to make my bed and went to sleep.

The next morning, when I got up, I stood in the company formation at reveille. That is when I saw the officer in charge was the same one that I talked to the day before. He was a Major and informed me I was fluent in reading, writing and speaking German. Since I was RA, I would be temporarily assigned to him. This kept me from going to Korea. Thank you Grandma Ida.

The next few days were spent filling out forms for my clearance, which would allow me to have access to classified documents. I was indoctrinated as to what my duties would be in my new organization.

Sometime in October, 1951, I was given a three-day pass. On a Friday morning, I hitchhiked into Indianapolis and took a bus to Chicago and then to Milwaukee. My mother married William Herz the week before, and had moved to Milwaukee. They showed me around Milwaukee. I liked what I saw.

I left Sunday to go back to Camp Atterbury arriving in the late afternoon. Monday morning, right after first formation, I went to the orderly room and changed my home address to Shorewood, WI.

I was now a Wisconsinite.

Return To Germany 1951-1954

—◈—

IN EARLY NOVEMBER, 1951, we departed for Germany via Philadelphia. The train took us to the Philadelphia Navy yard. We would be going overseas on the troop ship the USS Buttner.

First, we had to parade through the downtown area. I did not see too much of Philadelphia because I was in the middle ranks, but I recall marching down Market Street. The men in the forward ranks were yelling back to watch out for the horse manure.

We said good-bye to our friends and relatives who had come to see us leave. Aunt Edith and Grandma Ida were there to see me off.

The trip across was very unpleasant. Our bed was a pipe ring with a piece of canvas laced around the outer edges. Our duffle bags were stored at the bulkhead. My pillow was my helmet. My blanket was my over coat and I slept with my rifle. We were allowed two meals a day. The showers were of salt water, and very small.

Once we arrived in the open seas, it got a little rough and the ship rocked back and forth. Many troopers got sea sick, so I was able to wrangle meal cards from them, since I was not sick. The food was excellent but we had to stand up to eat by long tables with eight soldiers on each side. Sometimes, if the sea was very rough the trays would slide down to the other end and somebody might throw up in the food. This was not pleasant.

I volunteered to work and was assigned to the bow, forward, latrine as the NCO in charge. One day I had four cleaners working and as the ship experienced rough waves, two of the men were tossed about and one broke his arm.

There was not much to do aboard the ship. We did have PT led by the famous Philly's pitcher Curt Simmons until he got seasick, and threw up in his hat, which he threw over board. PT did not last too long.

The day before Thanksgiving, November 24, 1951, we landed in Bremahaven, Germany. I was summoned to the troop commanders' cabin where I was informed as to what my duties would be. I was to supervise the stevedores who were unloading the cargo. All of the cargo was in wooden crates and the corners were all painted in different colors corresponding to the organizations ownership.

I was on the deck when a stevedore boarded the ship and said to the others in German, "hey, look, here's a dirty Jew". That was my first encounter with a German in Germany since 1939. I ordered the stevedore off the ship and he lost his job. Another stevedore said, "Oh, he speaks and understands German". After that incident, I had no more difficulties with the unloading of the ship.

Being color blind, I had to ask someone what the colors were on the corners of the containers, as they had to be placed according to color on the pier. Everything went well. The Germans were polite and willing to do what I asked them to do, once they knew that I spoke German. They wanted to keep their jobs. During a break, I gave them cigarettes, which were hard to get. This really won them over, and one said, "He is one of the good guys. He does not hate us".

While on the pier, I asked myself what attitude I should have. Should I be angry at everyone or should I enjoy myself the few years that I would be in Germany before returning to the US? I made the right decision. I decided to enjoy myself, see as much as I could, and make the best of the situation, rather than being angry and hating everyone. I knew that I would have to work with the Germans, which would have been very difficult if I was angry with them. I would treat the Germans fairly, but firmly, learn as much as I could, and have a good time. I made friends, learned a great amount of history, and thoroughly enjoyed my tour. I have never regretted the decision.

General Eisenhower was there to greet us the next day. He gave an interesting speech and left us with a message that "we should conduct ourselves in such a manner that when we leave, people will say that they are sorry to see us go". This has been one of my guiding rules since that time and has stood me well all these years.

When I left Germany in 1954, the German mayor and police chief, with whom I had a close association, were sorry to see me leave. They gave me gifts, a parade in my honor and my favorite meal. I made a short speech where I said, "In 1939 I was forced to leave Germany; in 1954, you people are sad to see me leave"

Army Stories

———————— ⇒◇⇐ ————————

MY ATTITUDE TOWARDS GERMANS

As I was born in Germany, and having survived the rise of Hitler and Kristalnacht, it probably would appear to most people that I would have an inherent hatred of most Germans. I have always felt: NOT ALL GERMANS WERE NAZIS AND NOT ALL NAZIS WERE GERMAN.

My experience in the 1951-1954 period, where I was involved with the denazification process, gave me a deeper understanding of what a tyrannical government can do to its citizens.

In the time frame that I was stationed in Germany, it was a rare occurrence that I had to confront anti-Semitism besides the stevedore incident. I can recall one incident where, after raiding a house of prostitution, one of the ladies of the evening made an anti-Semitic comment, which resulted in her spending three months in the house of correction.

All in all, the period after WWII, as it affected me, was relatively free of bias.

THE FACTORY

In December of 1951, I went to Munich by train from Ellwangen to visit my relatives, Hans and Gretel Siegel. Because of Gretel being Jewish and Hans being Catholic, they had survived the war by being assigned to work camps. It was eerie coming into the railroad station that I had left twelve years earlier, at the age of seven, when fleeing for my life. The roof had been blown apart when bombs had hit Munich and this brought back bad memories.

I had wanted to visit the family greeting card factory so Hans arranged for me to talk to Mr. Herring, who now owned the factory, as he had purchased it from the family before they left for America, at a very reduced rate. This was a Gestapo forced sale. Mr. Herring was so surprised and happy to hear from me and immediately sent a car for me to come to the factory.

When I arrived at the factory, I followed a circular walkway to the front entrance and was surprised to see people standing at the entrance to greet me. These were the people who knew my father and remembered me as a little boy, who would visit his father, Max, in his office. I went into my fathers' office and was greeted by my fathers' secretary who still worked there. It was quite an emotional reunion when she saw me and wanted to know everything about me and my family, since we left Munich, what we did in America, how we were managing, and how Grandma Ida was, since my grandfather had founded the company.

After answering all her questions, one of the foremen came to take me on a tour of the factory. Everyone who had worked for my father stopped me to shake my hand and inquire about me and the family in America. I was invited for lunch at the director's table and everyone was very respectful to me. After lunch the tour continued, and then I returned to Hans and Gretel's' apartment.

Since it was such an emotional reunion, I vowed never to return. I saw what was suppose to be mine, one-day, and did not want to be reminded of that again. Today the factory is torn down. The business must have died out as they had old printing presses that no one would replace.

My thoughts: "I thought about how this would have been all mine, except for Hitler. Fate had different prospects for me. Now I am an American and a retired Army Colonel. I never would have achieved this rank in the German Army. So things worked out. I would have been wealthy in Germany; but I am grateful to be in the United States and have what I have. I cannot wish for the unattainable".

VISITING NOERDLINGEN – MAY 1952

I decided to take a trip to the home of my mother's ancestors – Noerdlingen. I caught a typical local train, a Bummelzug, in Ellwangen that would take me to Noerdlingen. There was a potbelly stove in the center of the train, but no restroom, because the train stopped at every little village along the way.

I was dressed in civilian clothes. I brought along a German newspaper to read on the trip. I had my ditty bag with me – toilet articles and a change of clothes since I planned to spend the night there. As the train was rumbling along the countryside, the conductor asked me for my ticket, which I surrendered to him. He asked me if I was an American Soldier. I replied that I was, and the conductor told me that I spoke good German and had an excellent Bavarian dialect.

He asked me why I was going to Noerdlingen and I told him about my family, that it was my grandmothers' hometown and that I was a descendant of the Marx family. The conductor was incredulous, because his mother had been a house cleaner for my great grandparents. The conductor invited me to stay with him at his house and wanted to show me Noerdlingen.

That evening the conductor's wife cooked dinner, potatoes, gravy, bread, and eintoff, leftovers, which were simmering on the wooden stove, something that every German did, simmer left overs, continuously.

I slept in the guest room, which faced the town square, in a big bed with a bloemo, feather bed. The next morning after breakfast, we started on our journey through the town. We went to the ruins of the old synagogue that was not rebuilt since there were no Jews living there anymore. We went to the cemetery, which had not been disturbed. We went to the large church, St. George, which the whole town had been built around. It was a Catholic church, and in the hallway were pictures of students who had attended the church school. Grandma Ida was one of the students. The conductor pointed out to me as many relatives of mine that he could remember.

Noerdlingen is a fortified town. It has a moat and a wall around it. The conductor told me about the towns history and how much destruction the war had done. I commented that it did not look like the war had been too bad on the town. The conductor answered, " Oh, yes, it was terrible". The enemy had surrounded the town and tried to starve the people out. The town was bombarded. I was shown a cannon ball imbedded in one of the four towers at each entrance. This was a round cannon ball and the conductors comment was that "this was from the thirty year war from 1618 to 1648". I asked "are you still fighting the war?" and he replied "we're not fighting anymore but it did a lot of harm to Noerdlingen".

We went to a house on the square and just walked right in. I was told that this was the Marx house. I saw the rooms where my aunts and uncles lived. Behind the house was a barn, now a bicycle sales and repair store. The present occupants of the house were very hospitable and were happy to see someone from the old days show an interest in the house. We went across the square to a stationary store to meet the owner. He was a classmate of my uncle. I later sent this mans name and address to Uncle Sigmund who was delighted to contact him.

I was impressed by the fact that my family had a nice house and I was allowed to tour the house to see where my great grandparents had lived. I was given a glimpse of the past.

When I returned to the United States and talked to my grandmother about my visit to Noerdlingen, she had left 50 years earlier and her memory was not so great any more, she was interested to hear how the rooms looked. She remembered the barn in the back where they had kept a horse and wagon. She asked about the synagogue and cemetery and what grave stones I saw, but I did not remember many of them, as they were not related.

Grandma Ida was in the pictures in the church and she was surprised that the pictures were still there. While still in Germany, the last time Grandma Ida had visited the church she had taken her two children, Thea and Edith, there.

SPANDAU PRISON

Spandau prison was located in Berlin and it was the prison for the Nazi war criminals. It was run by the US Army, the French Army, the British Army and the Russian Army. Each army was on a one month rotation running the prison. It was very old and was used by the Gestapo under the Nazi Regime. This also was where the conspirators, who attempted to kill Hitler, in July of 1944, were hung with piano wire.

Col McDonald of the American Army at the Stuttgart headquarters assigned me, in March, 1952, to work with the American Army for one month in the prison.

I arrived a day early and was briefed by Captain Ross about my duties.

He also informed me that as I was not a member of the Military Police Company, guarding the prisoners, I was not allowed to partake in the Changing of the Guard ceremonies but was allowed to be on the sidelines to watch this impressive ceremony.

Upon completion of Changing of the Guard ceremony, I was taken on an orientation tour of the prison, and the notable Nazi's incarcerated there were pointed out to me. They all seemed like docile old men. The only exception was Rudolph Hess who, I determined, was quite mad.

Rudolph Hess was Hitler's personal secretary. He was a pilot and was seriously wounded in WWI. In September of 1940, he took it upon himself to go to Augsburg and take a Messerschmitt ME109 single seat fighter and fly to England to arrange some type of cease-fire between Germany and Great Britain. He had to parachute out of his plane, which crashed and he was immediately captured and imprisoned.

My job entailed accompanying the Sgt of the Guard on his rounds, and interpreting for him what the prisoners' needs were.

I always wondered what the Nazis thought as they probably figured out I was a native born German. I used to watch Rudolph Hess in the middle of the inner courtyard, as he was allowed to have a garden. He would always get into a fight with the other prisoners and the guards would have to rescue his victims. I can remember one fight that he had with Speer. He was screaming that Speer stole his sticks for the tomatoes. Then he proceeded to beat him up. We solved the problem by replacing the sticks.

The food was very good, much too good for the prisoners who starved slave laborers and exterminated Jews.

I lived with other MP's in the barracks not far from the prison. We pulled eight-hour tricks, six days a week. We were on call for the seventh day, which meant that we would not see much of Berlin.

PROSTITUTES – ELLWANGEN

One of my first jobs in Ellwangen in June, 1952, was to run the vice squad. I would accompany the German Police on their rounds of checking prostitute ID cards. One day my adjutant, Captain Thomas Codamo told me to reduce the VD rate in the 103rd Engineers Battalion. I decided that the best way to do this was to eliminate the prostitutes.

I requisitioned a squad of nine men and two six by six trucks. Before I left the Muehlberg Kaserne, I told the men to pull off the tarp from the back of the trucks and remove the bows, and raise the benches.

We went to the two houses of prostitution. Inside I had the prostitutes remove their clothes, except for their shoes, thy were marched into the truck. They were driven through the town with the truck horns blaring and searchlights shining on them. They were taken to the police station.

What a surprised look on the faces of the policemen when 32 naked prostitutes were paraded into the police station. The next day the local newspaper carried the story "CONTONMENT NIGHTMARE STRIKES". That was me – the KASERNENSCHREK.

The prostitutes were fined ten marks and then were ordered by the judge to leave town. The VD rate dropped dramatically. Captain Codamo was happy, but not the GI's and the prostitutes.

Jail

July, 1952, the 103rd Engineers were to practice building bridges across the Danube as they maneuvered against the 43rd Infantry Division. I was ordered to put on civilian clothes, requisition a bicycle, and find out the disposition, strength, and equipment of the opposing engineer battalion.

As I was walking down the road in my civilian clothes, pushing my bicycle with no tires, a landespolizist, state trooper, accosted me and wanted some ID. I had none so I was taken to the nearest police station until they could determine who I was. I tried to explain to them that I was a German student, but they did not believe me, because I could not tell them the names of my teachers, so I told them that I was an American soldier.

They did not believe me then either since they said that my Swabish dialect was too good. They put me in a cell with a straw mattress, fed me some kind of onion soup and bread and turned off the light.

The next day, around noon, I heard English being spoken in the front of the police station, so I yelled and Lt Doyle Gibson heard me and got me out of jail. Needless to say, I was not happy. Lt Gibson had come to the police station to inquire if I had been in an accident, since he had missed me when I did not report in for supper the night before, and had decided to wait until the next day before looking for me. He thought I had had an accident on my lousy bike and that the police would know where I was. It took a few days before I could laugh about the incident.

VIENNA

March, 1953, I was ordered to report to the 796th MP battalion in the city of Vienna, Austria. I took the Mozart Express train for U.S. Army Personel only, from Munich, and arrived in Vienna after crossing through the Russian Zone of Austria.

When I arrived in Vienna, I was taken to the 796th MP Battalion headquarters stationed at the STIFTSKASERNE in downtown Vienna. Upon entering this garrison I noticed that it had a remnant of WWII, a Flakturm, an antiaircraft tower. When I walked into the station and looked at the desk Sgt I recognized him to be the former tenant, Lt Johnson, who roomed with the family in Hackensack, N.J. during WWII.

After catching up on personal news about each other, I went into a side room where I was given my assignment, walking around the Russian sector in civilian clothes in order to ascertain what the Austrians thought of Stalin's death. I was to call in every morning.

Nothing much happened and I decided no one really cared, which made me feel like I had not done too much. I did a lot of sight seeing, eating viener schnitzel, goulash, chicken paprika, and drinking good beer.

After a few days of this "boon doogle", I was re-assigned to a company called "The Four Power Patrol" which maintained order in Vienna. This patrol consisted of an American driver, and British, French, and Russian soldiers sitting inside a four-door Chevy sedan. Again, no eventful occurrence transpired.

I was ordered to return to my duty station in Ellwangen. As I was leaving the STIFFKASERNE, a Viennese taxi struck me. I went flying in one direction and my duffle bag went in another direction. This happened in front of a bierstube. The owner saw the accident and went inside to get a mug of beer for me. I was not hurt so I went on to the station to board the Mozart Express.

As I was traveling west along the Danube River, I noticed that the Russians had deployed various trucks, tanks, armored personal carriers and self-propelled howitzers. As I felt that I had not really accomplished much I decided, stupidly, to take pictures even though I had been warned not to take pictures of anything Russian.

When I arrived in Linz, the train stopped, which was unusual as the Mozart Express was a military train and was to have free access. A Russian Sgt climbed aboard the train, demanded my documents and told me "du kom". He was armed so I went with him. He took my camera and told me to go into a wooden hut next to the train tracks. Inside, a Soviet Lt opened my camera and exposed the film. I was then finger printed, photographed and interrogated for ninety minutes to determine whether or not I was a spy.

Finally another train came through heading for Salzburg. I was allowed to leave on that train, with my camera, and was told to never come back. When I arrived in Salzburg, my baggage was in the stationmaster's office. I phoned my commanding officer to inform him as to what had happened. My commanding officer told me to take the weekend off in Munich, which I did.

Prisoner Chasing In Rome

One day, in early June, 1953, Captain Gibson informed me that I was to go to Rome to pick up a prisoner. I do not recall what he did, but I was to bring him back to Ellwangen under guard. He was to be court marshaled.

I went to the arms room and drew a 45-caliber handgun, handcuffs and leg irons. I kept thinking that here I am, walking around with a 45 under my armpit and what if I was arrested. I did have orders authorizing me to be armed.

I went to the Ellwangen railroad transportation office and bought my ticket, round trip, from Ellwangen to Rome and back. I told the stationmaster that I was armed so I should have my own compartment. He told me that he was not authorized to give me that and I would have to travel second class. That really shocked me as I was bringing a prisoner back, in shackles, and handcuffed.

The train ride to Rome was uneventful and I arrived after an overnight trip, spent in that crowded second-class compartment. I immediately went to the police station to inform them that I had arrived. The police officer in charge asked me how long I wanted to stay in Rome. He would release the prisoner whenever I wanted him. I thought this was a pretty good deal. I do not recall the name of the hotel, where I stayed, but it certainly was not a five star hotel.

I proceeded to tour the city. I went to the Coliseum as well as some of the other Roman ruins. I went to Vatican City, the Spanish Steps, and the Tiber River.

After a few days of running around, I decided that I should take the prisoner back. He was released into my custody. I put the leg irons on him, which were attached to a chain around his waist. I put handcuffs on him. The police transported us to the railroad station. We had no food, which was probably my fault, since I did not know we would spend ten hours on the train. The train did not have a dining car.

Once again the compartment was crowded. I recall an elderly gentleman who spoke English, asking me what my prisoner did. I told him that he was a murderer. That almost emptied the compartment. The prisoner was not too happy. An elderly lady stayed and gave us bread and salami. The prisoner asked her what kind of salami it was and she answered "mule meat". We also had goat cheese. It was all very good but the prisoner did not like it.

We finally arrived in Ellwangen. I turned the prisoner over to Captain Codamo, who asked me if I enjoyed my holiday as I overstayed the time allocated to me.

POLES EXECUTED IN ELLWANGEN

One day, in the fall of 1953, I received a call from the Chief of Police, Hans Knoedl. He requested the US Army furnish him with some trucks and a squad of men. It appeared that out by our ammo dump, a mass grave was discovered containing 38 poles.

They came from the Ellwangen Concentration Camp and had been executed by the SS. Hans Knoedl wanted our people to disintern the victims, put their bodies on our trucks, take them to the cemetery, and give them a proper burial in a mass grave.

I was on very good terms with the Chief of Police. I informed him "under no circumstances would I request a truck or a squad of men". "They were killed by the SS and it is only fitting that they be taken care of by the Germans".

It then dawned on me that in my lowly position I was not authorized to make such a decision. I went to the Adjutant, Tom Codamo, and informed him that I had overstepped my authority in denying the Chief what he wanted. Tom looked at me and said, "You were absolutely right. We are not going to do that. But in the next couple of days, I want you to go out there, see what is going on, and report back to me".

About two days later, I went out there about noontime to see what they were doing. One of the gravediggers was sitting on the chest of a cadaver, eating his lunch. I nearly threw up. The other one was rummaging around in the pit looking for spent rounds. He offered me one, but I naturally refused it. I do recall the chief saying to me that I was right in turning him down.

I think he thought that I was part of the German Army not the American Army.

A few days later I was invited by the Chief to visit the mass grave that the Germans had established for these victims. Each victim was buried in his own casket.

Sad to say they had no way of identifying the victims. I requested that the gravesite have a tombstone and a bed of flowers. I was told that some time in the future when money was available, this would be done.

In 2007, Belle Anne, Mark, Laura, Philip, Jacqueline, Craig, Joseph, Samuel, Daniel and I went to Germany. On Saturday, Mark rented a car and took Belle Anne and I to Ellwangen. Just by chance we walked through the cemetery. Belle Anne noticed a grave that had a beautiful garden and a huge tombstone. She drew my attention to it and I realized that the promise had been kept.

TUNNEL

In late 1953, Col Mac Donald called me from the 66th CIC in Bad Canstadt telling me that I was going to Berlin. When I asked what I would be doing there, I was told just to report to CIC headquarters in Berlin.

When I reported in, I was told my duties would be to monitor telephone lines that had been intercepted in a junction box in a German cemetery. This telephone originated in the East German headquarters. My assignment was to monitor the transmissions and tape them on a wire recorder. When I heard certain words or phrases, I was to write down where they were located on the tape recorder and put it in brackets on the counter.

The tunnel was buried in a cemetery and was very damp and muddy, although later they did get duckboards. It was terribly odorific. I did this for 30 days, 4 hours on and 4 hours off. When I returned to my unit, I later heard that the tunnel had been discovered, due to snow falling that melted above the tunnel.

Many years later, Floyd Paxman informed me that his father-in-law, a CIA station chief in Berlin, had supervised this project. He also said that a mole in the headquarters of the four powers of Berlin had informed the Russians of the tunnels existence and therefore the East Germans would transmit fake information.

This made me very disappointed since I thought that I had been involved in a real intelligence coup. All that time sitting in that stinky tunnel was for naught. The Russians knew from the beginning that the tunnel existed.

Our Life by Belle Anne

Fifty years, what a life,
To be husband and wife.
Six hundred dollars we had.
We did not think that was so bad.
Phil was in the first graduating class of UWM.
It was June of 1957.
One week later we were married.
We were on top of the world.
We had met the previous September.
Phil was going to class.
I was selling tickets to the Theatre plays.
He bought a ticket and I went with him.

— BY BELLE ANNE
Written for our 50th wedding anniversary.

STATE TEACHERS COLLEGE became University of Wisconsin – Milwaukee in 1956, the year we met. Phil had started college in 1954, the year he was discharged from the army, and his tuition and books cost a staggering amount of $60 a semester. The cost elevated in 1956 when the tuition rose to $90 plus the cost of the books. Fortunately for Phil he was a senior and only had to pay this amount for one year. I was used to the higher amount since I had transferred to Milwaukee from UW-Madison where I already paid this amount the year before.

We met by the front door of Mitchell Hall, the only building that held the academic classes. I was involved with selling tickets for the theatre group that put on plays every other month of the school year. I helped with make-up and bookkeeping, and truly enjoyed my jobs with the theatre group.

We, who were part of the theatre group, had to spend time selling tickets to the students enrolled in the school. We had a good time meeting the students.

Phil walked by, or rather ran, to his class and did not want a ticket. He was late and had no time to talk. After his class he walked by our table again and had time to joke around a bit. He said he would buy a ticket if I would go with him and I said OK, since I had no one to go with anyway, except my roommates. It seemed to be more fun to accept this date.

Phil was an assistant manager and offered me a job being a marketier for the Milwaukee Sentinel newspaper selling subscriptions over the phone at night, for $1.50 an hour. I would work any night that I was available, for three hours each time. Since I was looking for a job I went to work and earned enough money to stay in school.

We established a wonderful relationship working, dating, and living from check to check. By December we were engaged, and we were married April 19th, by Judge Decker, in Milwaukee, and again June 23rd, by Rabbi Stauber, in Fond du Lac, WI.

We weathered hard times when we found out that jobs were hard to find. There was a recession going on and a lot of lay offs. Phil became a Fuller Brush Salesman and loaded up our apartment with bags full of orders from people he had solicited by going door to door in an assigned neighborhood. We also found out how hard it was to be a salesman when people refused to pay for their orders. So he made a job change.

Phil was an Army Reservist and was well liked in his unit. His commanding officer gave us a case of combat rations that was not needed. Another reservist hired him to be a carpenter's helper and that job lasted until the company folded, which came a few months later. During that time Phil made a toolbox, an end table, and a breadboard, which I kept forever until it wore out. He worked with formica, and learned what it was all about to work with ones hands.

By that time I was nearing the end of the semester. We had agreed that I should stay in school and graduate in education. I was hired by Herb Kohl. I worked one summer for Kohls grocery store to earn my tuition funds. I completed one semester of school. However, our roles were soon reversed, and we decided that Phil should become the student again and I should go to work full time. He had just been laid off from his carpenters' job because the company closed down.

Phil would be certified in Education and become a Junior High School teacher. I would become a Service Representative working for the Telephone Company where I stayed for almost three years until I became pregnant with our first child and we could afford to buy a house.

We bought our house in March of 1960 and Margarette was born in August of that year. We bought our dog Penny, a beagle, two weeks before I retired from my job and were anxious to bring her home, once I was home to care for her. She was a good dog but became too demanding once Mark was born in January of 1963, so we found a good home for her by giving her to friends of ours.

Our family continued to grow for the next few years. Perry was born in December of 1964 and Jacqueline came in September of 1966. I was a stay at home Mom which was also our plan. We did not have a lot of material things because we had mouths to feed and it all fell on Phil's shoulders to provide for us. He worked many jobs day and night and on weekends to take care of us.

The Army was a lifesaver since he was encouraged by special friends in the Army to apply to become an officer. He had gone to Army Intelligence School in the summer and placed first in his class. He would do two weeks of duty every summer during which time he could attend a military school. His instructors suggested that he apply for Second Lieutenant and return the next year on the Staff and Faculty of the Military Intelligence School and work with them.

Phil applied for Second Lieutenant and was turned down because he was too old. So he applied for First Lieutenant and was given a direct Commission in 1960. The next summer he had his teaching job with the Military that lasted for 23 summers. He would work for MPS, first as a teacher and later as a Counselor after getting his Masters in Counseling from Marquette University.

The summers were spent at various Military Bases, teaching most of the summer at Fort McCoy, and then doing two weeks with his assigned unit. He did not miss his time spent fixing roads, one of which was Lake Drive or working for Allis Chalmers as an open sand pit molder in the foundry. He has many scars where the melted steel hit his body.

My summers were lonely without Phil since we had to stay home, while Phil worked at Fort Sheridan, IL, and later Fort McCoy, WI. I enrolled our children in summer school and various other activities and they enjoyed themselves going to sport lessons, Scout day camp, of which I was assistant leader, library school, playground activities and playing in the neighborhood with the many children we had living around us. Our alley was wall-to-wall children at that time.

In 1969, our son Mark felt that we should have a puppy when his friend down the street had daschunds to sell, so Schatzie joined our family. When she was two she gave us six puppies, all born on her second birthday, February 2. We kept a male puppy, Snoopy, so that Schatzie would have company. They gave us many hours of entertainment.

In 1970, we bought a travel trailer to live in during Phil's time in Army summer camp and thus became camp followers. Wherever he went, we lived in our twenty-two foot, Pathfinder, trailer that we pulled with our car. We camped at various campgrounds near Fort McCoy and eventually on the grounds of Fort McCoy when a campground was opened up for the dependents.

Wherever we went, our children always made friends and enjoyed the local activities for children. They became excellent swimmers at the post pool and the two oldest ones earned Junior Life Saving Certificates before our time ended at Fort McCoy.

After his assigned time at Fort McCoy in the summer, Phil had his obligation to spend two weeks with his unit of assignment in Washington D.C. We packed up the trailer and drove fast to D.C. since most years he was released on a Saturday and had to be in D.C. by Sunday night with our trailer connected to water, electricity, and sewer before he could report to the Pentagon on Monday morning.

What a crazy time that was, but he always reported in on time. After that tour he had to hurry home to report in for his civilian job. We seemed always to be running from job to job.

In the meantime, the children and I toured D.C., saw all the buildings that were open for us to see, like the FBI Building, The State Department, The Supreme Court Judges Chambers, The White House, the Capitol, and the Smithsonian Museum that was housed in only one building at the time.

Sometimes we could meet Phil for lunch at the Forestal Building that was across the street from the Smithsonian. I would take Phil to work in the morning and pick him up late afternoon after work. We would frequent the military swimming pools of which there were many. We lived in trailer courts on Highway One, in Alexandria, VA, about thirty minutes from Phil's job.

Eventually, when Jacqueline started first grade, I investigated returning to UWM. It was time for me to take the leap, so I took one course, liked being back to school and continued until I graduated and was able to start working and helping to pay the bills. Phil could finally breath easier. Several years later I graduated from UWM with a Masters in Education. Phil had already received his Masters in Counseling in 1966 from Marquette University.

The years passed, the children grew up, graduated High School and or College, which ever was their choice, married and gave us eight grandchildren. Margarette became a nurse. Mark worked for Sears in Chicago as a Systems Analyst until he changed profession to become a Chiropractor, which involved more schooling. Today he has a clinic in IL. He married Laura, who is a Graphic Artist, as well as being a painter of flowers. Perry became an auto mechanic.

Jacqueline liked her job as a waitress, but also went to school to become a massage therapist. She married Craig, who is a tool and die specialist as well as a computer specialist in his field. We have very productive children and are proud of their achievements.

The time came when we retired from MPS, and Phil, from the Army. Phil chose to work three more years for the Whitnall School System as a Counselor before he started his next career as a volunteer Police Officer. It took me a year to finally enjoy my retirement. I missed the activities of the school where I taught children with Learning Disabilities. The staff was wonderful to work with and I missed the friendships that I had developed.

I took a quilting class, a painting class and a sign language class and gradually started a new life. I also started my volunteer work at St. Michael's hospital, as well as various other volunteer jobs. Three years later Phil was totally retired and we could spend more time together. It did not take him long to find volunteer jobs that he liked, with the Whitefish Bay Police Dept, and the VA.

Phil had always said that one day we would travel. The day came and he bought time-shares that I always thought he was against owning. We have been to so many more places than we ever dreamed of going to because of that purchase.

We took the family to Munich to see where Phil lived until he had to leave at the age of seven. We also toured most of Munich and other places in Germany and Austria. It was a wonderful trip and Phil was happy to guide our family around. Everyone enjoyed listening to him speak German to the natives. The food was wonderful and the pretzels were bigger than any one had ever seen. Phil's father is buried in Munich. We paid homage to him. The whole trip had an emotional effect on everyone.

Because of his experience during the Holocaust, Phil has many speaking engagements every year so that the Holocaust is not forgotten. This is his personal mission. I attend all of these engagements with him. Our children join us when they can. They are the ones who will have to carry on this message when we no longer can.

"Voyage of the Damned"
Recalled by 5th USAIS Dept Chief

———————— ⇒⋄⇐ ————————

AUGUST 18, 1977

BY ROBERT GIBLIN AS REPORTED IN THE CAMP MCCOY TRIAD

Many people have had personal experiences which taught valuable lessons, but few have had experiences with as much social and historical impact as Lt Col. Phillip Freund, director, tactical intelligence department, Fifth U. S. Army Intelligence School. At the age of eight, Freund became one of 937 Jews exiled from Germany on the passenger ship St. Louis... a ship crossing more commonly known as the "Voyage of the Damned."

Most people are reluctant to relate such experiences of war and persecution – not Freund. He feels that this type of thing should not be forgotten. "If it's buried in the past," he remarked. "it could happen again."

He continued, "I feel that people, especially young people should be educated as to the terrible things that can be done through inhumanities. There's an old saying, "If we don't study history, we're doomed to repeat it."

Freund related this philosophy to his own field of military intelligence. "With intelligence, we have to learn the mistakes of the past – and not make them again."

The exact story of the St. Louis voyage is both detailed and complicated. Freund related his shortened version of the story this way...

"When Hitler was gaining power in Germany, he wanted to prove a point that the Jews would not be welcome anywhere, so he allowed 937 to leave on a passenger ship. The St. Louis sailed from Hamburg in 1939, under the command of a Capt. Schroeder. Their destination was Havana, Cuba, where they expected to be granted freedom. It was unknown to the captain, crew, and passengers that they wouldn't be welcomed, or allowed to debark in Cuba.

All we knew, when we arrived in Cuba, was that we couldn't get off the ship and get the safe haven we were longing for. We didn't know why, and didn't learn about the situation until we were in England.

The ship left Cuba and anchored outside of Miami Beach, until we were driven off by the Coast Guard. From there we sailed to Antwerp, Belgium. We were there for two days.

In Antwerp, the passengers were divided into four groups. The groups were let off in four different countries: France, Belgium, Holland, and England.

We were sent to Yelverton, England, where we stayed until December.

We landed in America on Christmas Eve, 1939. I was amazed at the number of bright lights. The war was escalating in England when we left, so the lights were kept low, and were shut off whenever possible."

That about ended Freund's tale of the "Voyage of the Damned." He then moved to Hackensack, N.J. The life style there was a far cry from that of his home in Germany. All that is left of that home is a memory. His German home was down the street from a Kaserne. He remembers the track vehicles, marching troops, and the tremendous feelings of hostility and anxiety.

Freund enlisted in the U.S. Army in 1951, immediately after graduating from high school. This began his long and interesting career in the intelligence field.

While on active duty, his job was to interrogate Sudeten Germans, native Germans who crossed the Iron Curtain out of Czechoslovakia. Freund helped to ascertain whether or not they were bonafide refugees.

Freund left the Army to attend college, but remained active in the U.S. Army Reserve. As a reservist he worked his way through the enlisted ranks to the grade of E-8. He received his commission in 1960.

Freund is as serious about teaching students in the 5th USAIS about intelligence as he is about relating his voyage on the St. Louis.

"This is a tactical school that emphasizes gathering and collecting information," Freund explained. "We teach our students to be the eyes and ears of commanders. Our philosophy here is that we're training people to save lives."

The colonel continued, "In a combat situation it's imperative that commanders know what they're facing. Otherwise it would be like putting a boxer into a ring with a mask over his face – he can't win!"

Like many other staffers at the 5th USAIS, education is Freund's civilian profession. He is a guidance counselor at the Wells Street Junior High School in Milwaukee.

He also makes his home in Milwaukee, with his wife, Belle Anne, and Four children; Jacqueline, 11; Perry, 13; Mark, 15; and Margarette, who celebrates her 17th birthday today.

1994 Documentary

In September of 1993, I received a phone call from Maziar Bahari, in Canada, asking me if I was interested in participating in a documentary of the St. Louis saga. This was in conjunction with Galafilm of Canada as well as the Canadian Broadcasting Corporation. This subject was of interest to him and he wanted to inform the public about it.

I advised him that I would participate and he said that he would like to interview me. Several weeks later he came to my home and we had a pleasant visit. He asked me many questions about my experience concerning the St. Louis.

In March of 1994, Maziar informed me that I had been selected to be a participant in the documentary production. I then informed him that I would be delighted to participate but requested that my wife accompany me. He approved my request. We would be on a cruise for seven nights and eight days.

On May 21, 1994, we left Milwaukee and flew to Miami. Sol Messinger was at the airport when we arrived and he introduced himself to us as a survivor and a Pathologist from Buffalo, New York. I must have looked like a survivor of the MS St. Louis since he had approached us and asked us if we had the same destination as he. We immediately took a liking to each other.

Seven survivors were already on the Italian cruise ship, the 'American Adventure'. When we got to the dock, the film crew was ready to film us boarding the ship. We were the last to arrive of the nine participants to be filmed. We were introduced to Herb Karliner who was waiting to greet us. He was the spokesman for the group. He took us to a room where the others were congregating and in the process of establishing friendships. This was our first meeting since 1939 and no one recognized each other.

Gisela Feldman and Sonia Sternberg, sisters from England, were happy to meet us, as well as the others, Anna Fuchs-Marx, the oldest one, Suzanne Schleger, Harry Rossbach, and Liesl Loeb. Additional family members accompanied some of the participants. Our first encounter went very smoothly as we all felt a kinship and were very grateful that Maziar had brought us together.

As the ship was departing, we sat down to dinner and soon half of the dining room was empty due to seasickness. Hans Oohms, the soundman, and I were the only ones left at our table. The film crew consisted of eight people.

Several individual interviews were scheduled with each participant. We were interviewed by Terence McKenna in a private room. We also had group discussions several times. We enjoyed finding out that we, the survivors, shared the same concerns.

The next morning, after breakfast and on the high seas, we commenced being filmed until after we docked in Nassau. We responded to questions. We expressed our feelings upon leaving Germany. There had been a band at the dock when we left Germany that played the song "Must I leave my little village". This memory made us very sad.

We discussed our departure from Germany and the Nazi regime. We had been looking forward to establishing a new life somewhere. We did not know what was in store for us in Cuba and eventually the US where my mother, and others on the ship, had quota numbers. Our belongings consisted of two suitcases and 10 marks ($4.20) per person.

The next day we arrived at a private island off the Dominican Republic shores. Filming was done continuously and it was interesting to note that the other passengers on the ship were interested in what we were doing. Some thought that we were movie stars. During the filming we discussed our lives under the Nazi's, how we were persecuted, as well as what happened to us once we left the MS St. Louis.

We left the Dominican Republic and preceded west, past the Cuban coast where we saw the lights of the homes of the people living along the shore-line. We were still on the outside looking in. We ended up in Key West where we got off the vessel and walked along the main street. We ate a section of frozen chocolate covered key lime pie on a stick. It was delicious.

Shortly afterwards, we reboarded the vessel and returned to the Miami Harbor where we disembarked and were taken to a hotel suite for the continuation of the filming. From then on the filming was done at the Miami South Beach Holocaust Memorial where we spent a full day filming. Herb Karliner was one of the charter members of this memorial.

We were there on Memorial Day and held a service for the Jewish victims of the Holocaust. I read my prayer. Then Sol Messinger led us in Hebrew prayers. We also prayed for those deceased American Military Personnel. I wore my full dress blues military uniform.

After the filming we returned to the Crown Sterling Suites Hotel to say our sad good-byes. We hoped that we would meet again one day and agreed to keep in touch.

Belle Anne and I returned to Milwaukee, proud of my accomplishments. At that point I decided to retire from my counseling position with the Whitnall School System.

Eventually, I received a copy of the documentary and was able to use it during my speaking engagements to students and adults. It was well received. It has been shown on TV in Europe, the US and the Western Hemisphere.

This documentary remains in my home library of cassettes as well as in the video collection at the Military Intelligence School at Fort Huachuca, Arizona, to be viewed by the Officer Orientation students. It is used to show the students what events occurred in 1939 and its impact upon the "Final Solution", the murder of six million Jews and six million others.

St. Louis Survivor Reunions

OUR FIRST REUNION ~ CANADA

In November of 1999, Herb Karliner contacted us to ask if I would be interested in attending a reunion of the St. Louis survivors in Ottawa, Canada. A Christian Evangelical group led by David Damien would sponsor this gathering.

Upon our arrival in Ottawa at the airport, in March of 2000, we were greeted by the sponsors of this reunion. They assisted us with our baggage and conveyed us to the hotel. This was the first time that we met other survivors who were not involved in making the 1994 documentary.

We were given a tour of the city, and later attended a banquet in a revolving restaurant located at the top of the hotel. We had a beautiful view of the city. We also had time to socialize with our fellow survivors and the hosts as well.

We were housed in a beautiful older hotel and later participated in a service where the Canadians pleaded for our forgiveness. This included the archbishop of Canada, native Canadians, the Chief Rabbi of Ottawa, and government officials from both Canada and the Ottawa Province.

The temper of the times in 1939 was such that the Canadian Minister of Immigration made the comment that "None is too many". There is a book called NONE IS TOO MANY, written by Irving Abella and Harold Troper. Both were professors of history in Toronto in 1983. The book was published by Random House.

We gathered in a private room to discuss our involvement with the Christian group. Dr David Damien bared his soul, telling us why he gave up a very lucrative medical practice. He felt that apologies had to be made to the survivors of the St. Louis in order for Canada to begin a healing process.

He emotionally begged for our forgiveness, as did others of his group, including Rosemary Schindler, a relative of Oscar Schindler.

The emotions were very high as survivors began to speak. My emotions were brought to the surface. We had never been requested for forgiveness and were so impressed by their compassion and empathy for the victims of the St. Louis.

That evening, a large banquet was held in our honor. After many speeches requesting forgiveness, we dined in a magnificent dining room and some of the survivors were asked to address the audience, I being one of them.

I remember telling the audience "we can easily forgive you because you are not the perpetrators and we do not hold the offspring of the perpetrators responsible for that which occurred. We will never forget that we were denied entry into Canada and we will continue to recite the Kaddish for those who died".

Canadians again asked for redemption. A high school choir sang songs. A group preformed a play. At the conclusion of the banquet, each survivor in attendance was presented with a glass sculpture depicting outstretched hands supporting the Star of David and the MS St. Louis passing through its center and resting on a maple leaf, the symbol of Canada.

Teary good-buys were said and hopes were expressed that we would meet again.

The next morning Belle Anne and I were taken to the airport by a Lt Commander of the Canadian Forces.

Our Second Reunion ~ Florida

In early June of 2001 we again had a reunion of the survivors of the MS St. Louis, sponsored by our Christian friends, led by Tom Hess, of Mount of Olive, Jerusalem.

Our son, Mark, contacted his siblings about joining us, after he had talked to Rosemary Schindler, secretary to Tom Hess. He was very interested in being a part of this event and she was very positive about additional family members joining this group. Our daughter, Jacqueline, came with Mark. They flew to Florida with us.

This reunion was held in Fort Lauderdale, Florida. Once again our Christian friends assisted us in getting to the hotel. That evening, we had a welcome program, which was held in a tent on the grounds of the hotel. The program consisted of many Christians, about 400 from various Central and South American Countries. They marched through the tent carrying large banners with Jewish symbols on them. Once more we were asked for their forgiveness for not letting the passengers disembark on their soil in order to be saved.

We held religious services, and showed the Canadian reunion film, as well as the documentary made in 1994. The documentary was shown again the next morning for those who had not seen it the previous night. We attended many meetings. Wherever we walked, people stopped us to beg for forgiveness, including a small nun from Germany.

It was at this time that we met some Jews for Jesus, who were part of our survivors group. David Damian informed these people that this was not acceptable. Proselytizing was unacceptable. We were not invited to this function to be encouraged to change our religion. They stopped.

The next day was June 5th, my birthday. We went to the estuary, at Fort Lauderdale, where the Coast Guard Cutter originated, in 1939, and had forced us to depart for international waters. We threw red roses into the water and held a service for those who died.

Upon our arrival at the hotel for lunch Tom Hess, sitting at my table, asked me where we should have the next reunion. I responded "Israel". He looked at me and replied, "we had just mentioned that location". Suddenly a beautiful birthday cake was put in front of me. What a pleasant surprise. In 1939, my mother told me that it was my birthday, but she was too disturbed to even mention it to anyone. This made up for the cake I did not receive in 1939 on the ship.

We were given baskets of goodies and a few of us received homemade teddy bears. This would come in handy when I had open-heart surgery.

The next morning we returned to Milwaukee.

In March of 2002, we flew to Newark, New Jersey where we boarded the Lufthansa flight to Frankfort, Germany. That would be the first time that Belle Anne set foot in Germany.

A group of German Christians greeted us at the airport and gave us food, flowers and drinks. We then flew to Hamburg where again we were greeted by a sizeable group of Christians who took us to the hotel close to the harbor. There were twelve survivors that attended.

The next day, we went to the Hamburg seat of government where we were welcomed and given some cake and coffee. The leaders received a key to the city, including Herb Karliner.

We walked to the harbor where we dedicated the plaque that was already in place, commemorating the tragedy of the MS St. Louis. The German government sent a representative to participate. We then went out into the harbor on lighters where we again held a ceremony, threw red roses into the water, sang songs and offered prayers.

While walking back to the hotel, a German gentleman spoke to me and stated that we are a remarkable group of people, as we harbored no hatred of the Germans. I replied that we cannot and will not hold responsible the offspring of the perpetrators.

We visited the grave of Captain Schroeder and said a prayer for him. We were thankful that he cared about us and did not return the St. Louis to Germany where we would have met our death.

That afternoon we had a meeting and Reverend Jorge Diaz pleaded for forgiveness and prostrated himself on the floor, as others had done before him. He then informed us that he wanted to take us to Cuba. He had left Cuba in 1980 with the Mariel boat people.

That evening we ate in the hotels' restaurant and then attended a play by High School students.

Early the next morning we departed Germany via Frankfort, arriving in Tel Aviv at noon, where we connected with Jacqueline in the airport. Mark joined us later that day in Jerusalem.

That day we were given a tour of Jerusalem and then went to the home of Tom Hess for lunch. After lunch and a ceremony, we went to the old portion of Jerusalem to shop for Judaican items. We also went to David's tomb, which we did not tour because I had been pick pocketed and my wallet was missing.

When we had left Tom Hess's house, some venders were outside on the street with a car trunk open and full of items to sell. A camel was there as well as a donkey. A man shoved a poster on my chest and reached into my fanny pack and took my wallet. He moved swiftly and I did not know that anything was wrong until later. I was very upset. Not only had he taken my visa card and drivers license, but he also took my military ID, and $200.

The people that we were with were so compassionate towards me. They took up a collection and gave me $200. When Mark joined us later in the day, he gave me his charge card and offered me some money, which I declined to take.

The following day we were invited to participate at a Bedouin luncheon, and some of us were treated to a camel ride. I watched while Belle Anne, Mark and Jacqueline had their ride. My heart surgery had been September 7, 2001 and I was not ready for this kind of experience.

When we went to the Dead Sea Hotel, my new Visa card was waiting for me, via Federal Express. Some of the group went swimming in the salty waters of the swimming pool in the hotel. One of the men fell into the salty water and had to have his eyes flushed out with fresh water before he had a permanent injury to them.

That evening we participated in enjoying a very magnificent buffet. The following morning we boarded the bus that took us sight seeing along the Jordan River where we stopped at Lake Tiberius. We had the local fish for dinner at a Kibbutz Nof Ginosar. We took a trip up to the Golan Heights where we could see what a strategic importance this location had.

We went on a bus tour of Northern Israel, stopping at the heights above the Bahai Gardens. Some of our Christian friends decided to blow their shofars. This created a stir among the Bahai worshippers and we were asked to leave.

That evening, in out hotel, we were again honored by a banquet and speeches. Sunday we departed for home.

In May, 2004, we departed Milwaukee for Miami and rented a hotel room near the airport.

The next morning we were picked up and taken to the Miami Airport where we met Mark and Jacqueline. Jorge Diaz was there to look after the eleven survivors of the St. Louis and our families who came along, 43 in all. He gave us our plane tickets, visas and nametags. It took three hours to go through customs and 65 minutes to fly to Havana.

Upon arriving in Cuba we went through customs and showed our passports. It was very hot and humid. Doney, our guide and George, our bus driver were waiting to take us to Hotel Nacional where we checked in and had lunch.

Our room was very warm so I asked the maid, in my limited Spanish, to make it cooler. She must have thought that I said it was too cold because she made it warmer for us for the duration of our stay. Mark and Jacqueline had a cool room and offered to trade with us, but we declined.

We were given a tour of Havana and ended up at El Moro Castle where we had a beautiful view of the city. We were allowed to take pictures. That evening, after dinner, we went to a private room where we held our own gathering.

The next morning we participated in a tour of the city of Havana, which included the Jose Marte Memorial Museum, the highest point in Havana. It is here, in the square, where Fidel Castro spoke to massive crowds.

We paid our respects at the Ashkenazic cemetery, located in a suburb of Havana, Wananvacoa. The first Holocaust Memorial in the Western Hemisphere is located in this cemetery. Across the street was the Sephardic cemetery, which we did not visit.

We returned to the hotel and met on the veranda where Mark kept supplying us with mojitos. We met Susan Forrest by accident. She did not know that we would be in Cuba. She had interviewed me in Fort Lauderdale Florida. She was still working on her film and we all agreed to be filmed by her at the hotel. Everyone enjoyed a Cuban cigar.

We relaxed until it was time to go to the synagogue where we held a Jewish service. The synagogue had been remodeled in 1950 using private funds from Cuban Jews living in Florida. It was beautiful except for the bathrooms in the basement that were holes in the floor. In 1960 there were 15,000 Jews in Cuba. 90% left. In 2004, there were 1500 in Cuba, 400 in Havana with about 40 families belonging to this synagogue.

A rabbinical student and two cantors led the service. An assembly representative, who worked with Fidel Castro, was there to offer somewhat of an apology. He wrapped Herb Karliner in a Cuban flag and Herb wrapped him in an Israeli flag. Jorge presented each survivor with a beautiful plaque and a pin with the Cuban flag on it.

After the service we returned to the hotel to have a delicious buffet. We ate very well.

The next day we went to a market, which was held one day a week, and bought souvenirs. Mark and Jacqueline wanted to explore the city on their own. We were told that they would be in no danger. They took a buggy ride. They ate at a Cuban restaurant and had delicious Cuban food. They met up with us after our lunch of hotel buffet.

We saw a lot that day of Havana. Some of the sights were: Revolution Square where Fidel held speeches, Pictures of Che Guevera, The National Art Museum, and The Revolutionary Museum where I was not allowed to take pictures, so I went to the air conditioned tobacco store and waited for Belle Anne.

Miriam, not a survivor, but an interested party, was born in Cuba and left in 1960. As a young girl she worked in Old Havana Square. She showed us the building and retraced the walks she had in the square. This was a very emotional time for her.

We went to San Francisco Square by the harbor near the arts and crafts market where people were allowed to sell homemade items only on Saturdays. We bought a few things. We walked down narrow alleys and streets and saw how poorly the people lived. We went through the historical Havana section and stopped at Hotel Rachel where we saw a picture of the MS St. Louis hanging inside on a wall.

We walked along the Prada and found the place where Jack and his sister Beatrice Sichel stayed with their parents before coming to the US. It was now an empty lot. This family was part of the 30 passengers who were allowed to leave the St. Louis in 1939 because they had legal papers.

Saturday night, after our banquet, we met and I read my thank you speech in Spanish. Everyone clapped, laughed, and hooted so much that I had to read it again. They were delighted that I took the time to compose a speech in a language that was most foreign to me. I was so grateful for being brought to Cuba. This time I was on the inside looking out and what a strange feeling it was. If only...

During our visit, we were never in any danger. If someone had bothered us they would have been arrested immediately. The soldiers were not visible but we knew that we were watched and protected.

Our Fifth Reunion ~ Miami

Many years previously, Rosemary Schindler spoke to me about getting an apology from the US Government for our inability to disembark from the MS St. Louis in 1939. Many times she, as well as Herb Karliner and I tried to obtain some type of recognition for the injustices meted out to us.

It was not until October of 2008, when Belle Anne and I were attending a reunion of the AFIO, Association of Former Intelligence Officers, in Washington DC that something finally happened. We were on the elevator in the US Capitol when Senator Herb Kohl of Wisconsin entered the elevator and stood in front of Belle Anne. She recognized him and told him that we would be bringing our family to DC in the summer. He told us to write to him and he would provide us with the necessary tickets for various places of interest.

Senator Kohl sent us tickets and an invitation to his breakfast. At his breakfast he greeted each family. When he came to our family, Belle Anne mentioned to him that I was a survivor of the MS St. Louis. He wanted to know more about this and put me in touch with his Chief of Staff, who asked if there was anything he could do for me.

I requested an apology from the US Government for not letting our ship land in the US and saving the lives of 907 passengers, six million Jews and six million others. It would have shown the Nazi's that there were countries that cared, and they would not have started the death camps

In April, 2009, I received a call from the Senators aide informing me that he had good news and bad news. The bad news was that there would be no apology. The good news was that a resolution was being considered in the Senate commemorating the 70th anniversary of the rejection of 907 passengers fleeing Nazi Germany. The resolution passed unanimously on May 26, 2009, Senate Resolution S111.

Senator Herb Kohl presented the resolution to me on June 6, 2009, standing near the fireplace in the Pfister Hotel in downtown Milwaukee.

I informed Rosemary Schindler and Herb Karliner that we had the resolution.

A reunion was planned to take place in Miami, Florida, in December of 2009. Mark and Jacqueline accompanied us.

The thirty-three survivors, who attended, signed copies that were sent out to 29 groups.

Several newspapers interviewed us and our stories were recorded on DVDs. I was on CNN December 13th. I was quoted in the Miami Herald December 14 as well as several other newspapers. My story was on the Internet.

We were treated very well by our sponsors. It was a wonderful reunion. It was a time to renew old friendships and meet new friends. Some of those in attendance had never been to a reunion before, even though they were all invited. They regretted not having come to the others.

A play was presented one evening, written by Robert Krakow, one of the sponsors of this reunion. It was called "The Trial of FDR" and I was one of the jurors.

Monday night we were invited to a reception sponsored by the Jewish Federation in Boca Raton. Robert Krakow presented his play "The False Witness: The Trial of Adolph Hitler.

On Tuesday, December 15th, The Greater Miami Jewish Federation invited us to a dinner to honor the remaining eleven survivors that were still in Miami. It was a very elegant affair.

We hope that this is not the final reunion, and that there will be others. We do not want to lose contact with our fellow survivors.

The website where the reunion can be viewed is www.thestlouisproject.com.

Resolution

May 26, 2009

RESOLUTION WOULD RECOGNIZE M. S. ST. LOUIS TRAGEDY

THE SENATE HAS PASSED A RESOLUTION SPONSORED BY SENATORS KOHL
(D-WI), VOINOVICH (R-OH), BROWNBACK (R-KS) AND
WYDEN (D-OR) THAT RECOGNIZES JUNE 6TH, 1939 AS ONE OF THE MOST
SHAMEFUL DAYS IN AMERICAN IMMIGRATION HISTORY.

THE TEXT OF S. RES. 111:

Recognizing June 6, 2009, as the 70th anniversary of the tragic date
when the M.S. St. Louis, a ship carrying Jewish refugees from Nazi Germany,
returned to Europe after its passengers were refused admittance to the United
States.

Whereas on May 13, 1939, the ocean liner M.S. St. Louis departed from
Hamburg, Germany for Havana, Cuba with 937 passengers, most of whom
were Jewish refugees fleeing Nazi persecution;

Whereas the Nazi regime in Germany in the 1930s implemented a
program of violent persecution of Jews;

Whereas the Kristallnacht, or Night of Broken Glass, pogrom of
November 9 through 10,

1938, signaled an increase in violent anti-Semitism;

Whereas after the Cuban Government, on May 27, 1939, refused entry
to all except 28 passengers on board the M.S. St. Louis, the M.S. St. Louis
proceeded to the coast of south Florida in hopes that the United States would
accept the refugees;

Whereas the United States refused to allow the M.S. St. Louis to dock
and thereby provide a haven for the Jewish refugees;

Whereas the Immigration Act of 1924 placed strict limits on immigration;

Whereas a United States Coast Guard cutter patrolled near the M.S.

St. Louis to prevent any passengers from jumping to freedom;

Whereas following denial of admittance of the passengers to Cuba, the United States, and Canada, the M.S. St. Louis set sail on June 6, 1939, for return to Antwerp, Belgium with the refugees; and

Whereas 254 former passengers of the M.S. St. Louis died under Nazi rule: Now, therefore, be it

Resolved, That the Senate —

(1) recognizes that June 6, 2009, marks the 70th anniversary of the tragic date when the M.S. St. Louis returned to Europe after its passengers were refused admittance to the United States and other countries in the Western Hemisphere;

(2) honors the memory of the 937 refugees aboard the M.S. St. Louis, most of whom were Jews fleeing Nazi oppression, and 254 of whom subsequently died during the Holocaust;

(3) acknowledges the suffering of those refugees caused by the refusal of the United States, Cuban, and Canadian governments to provide them political asylum; and

(4) recognizes the 70th anniversary of the M.S. St. Louis tragedy as an opportunity for public officials and educators to raise awareness about an important historical event, the lessons of which are relevant to current and future generations.

Baggage

PRESENTED AT CONGREGATION EMANU-EL B'NE JESHURUN
ON YOM HASHOA, APRIL 11, 2009, BY PHILIP S. FREUND

Good evening ladies and gentlemen.

Tonight we commemorate the annihilation of 2/3 of European Jewry. That translates to six million Jews and six million others. We have an obligation to never forget these poor souls, because if we do, then the murderers will have achieved their goal of making Europe "Judenfrei". What a symbolic tragedy that would be.

How did these atrocities affect the survivors? What baggage are we carrying around? What is the effect upon our daily lives, and our children and grandchildren's lives? Do we forever see ourselves as victims, even after sixty plus years later?

Sad to say there were many who could not cope with their experiences and they suffered mightily. My own mother never recovered from my fathers' execution, and until her own demise, lived in a world of sadness and guilt. She was bolstered by Valium.

She did enjoy her grandchildren.

I was born in Munich, Bavaria, Germany in 1931 to a family that lacked nothing, even during the 1920's. My father, Max Joseph, wanted to be a professional soldier and he participated in WWI as an Infantry Officer. My mother, a twin, was born in Munich and had close ties to her extended family. They were married in 1928 in Munich.

In 1933, Hitler was elected to the Legislature. In 1937, my father decided that we had to leave Germany and was in the process of starting a firm either in Sweden or Holland. He took some of the firms money to Holland. The Gestapo, during his absence, decided to audit the books and found discrepancies. My mother was arrested and held hostage. My father returned to Germany with the funds and was promptly executed.

My mother carried the scars of not insisting harder that we leave Germany earlier and she blamed herself for his death.

In 1935, in the city of Nurenberg, the Racial Laws were passed which deprived Jews of their citizenship and also imposed many restrictions and deprivations, i.e. restricted travel, blocked bank accounts, forced people out of civil service positions, confiscation of vehicles, radios, guns, binoculars, second homes and more.

On November 9, 1938, Kristalnacht occurred. We were home. I was playing with my train set while my mother was busy at the back of our home. The door bell rang, and I assumed that it was my grandmother, who lived around the corner, therefore, I went to answer the door. It turned out to be a Gestapo agent. He inquired about my father. When I told him that he was dead, he assaulted me and then picked me up to throw me against the wall. He was about to stomp on me when my mother, who had heard the commotion, came running and informed him that her husband was deceased. She showed him the legal document, and he left, all the while uttering profane comments.

This was not my first encounter with the Nazis. I was expelled from school at the age of six and beaten by a group of Hitler Jugend. Then I started the Jewish School but, during Kristalnacht, it was torched.

We were hidden at my father's platoon sergeant's farm until things quieted down. This was very brave of this ex soldier to do. If the Nazis had found out about this they would have killed him and his family, burned down his house and killed his cattle.

Upon our return to Munich, my mother learned that Cuba was allowing Jews to seek refuge there for the cost of $500 a person. The Hamburg-America line also sold round trip tickets to go on the MS St. Louis ship. My mother purchased four necessary documents (for my grandmother, sister, me and her). This was to be a temporary layover prior to emigrating to the US.

As we were making preparations to depart our home in Munich, my mother informed me that I could fill two suitcases only with clothes and take one toy. Imagine a seven year old having to leave my favorite things, including my bed and never again to see Paula, my governess, and Anna, our cook. This had a huge affect upon me. All of my things were going to be taken over by some Hitler Jugend. My beloved Paula and Anna would be gone. It left a huge hole in my psyche.

When we finally arrived in Cuba we were not allowed to disembark. It seems that the Cuban official had misappropriated the funds and therefore the entry permits were invalid. This gave us all trepidation as to why we were not accepted. Was it because we were Jews? Fortunately our family finally ended up in Great Britain.

After September 1, 1939, we were considered enemy aliens and had to leave London.

We finally arrived in the US December 24, 1939. My mother informed me that she could not provide for me and I had to stay in New Jersey with my aunt and uncle. I never really felt that I was a full fledged member of that family. They would spend the summer at the beach and I would go to the chicken farm to work. My cousins got bikes. I did not. It really left me with a lot of negative feelings. My uncle informed me on numerous occasions that in the future I would have to take care of my family.

While attending State Street Elementary School in Hackensack, my friend George Coty had asked me if I had a library card. I informed him that I had no money and that I was Jewish. He was flabbergasted, but took me anyway to the library. I still was not convinced that I was eligible for a card. When the librarian inquired as to our requests I again said that I had no money and was Jewish. She had difficulty understanding why I told her that I was Jewish with no money. I had a deep fear of being treated badly as I was Jewish.

All in all the major concern of us survivors is acceptance. We have this great fear of rejection. How does one eliminate this baggage? One must learn to accept one's self. Once a person has the aura of self worth and being able to make a contribution, the acceptance will follow.

I am so grateful to this nation for having finally accepted us and given us the opportunity to make a contribution and to become unimpeded citizens.

Thank you.

Direct Lineage Family Tree of Philip Freund

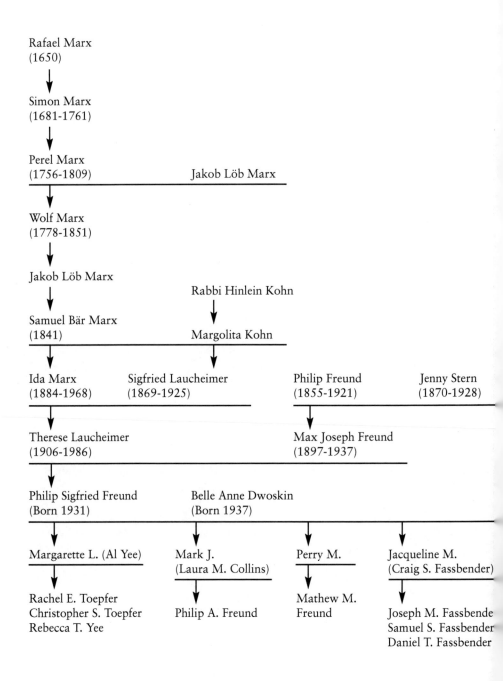

Rafael Marx
(1650)

Simon Marx
(1681-1761)

Perel Marx
(1756-1809)

Jakob Löb Marx

Wolf Marx
(1778-1851)

Jakob Löb Marx

Samuel Bär Marx
(1841)

Rabbi Hinlein Kohn

Margolita Kohn

Ida Marx   Sigfried Laucheimer   Philip Freund   Jenny Stern
(1884-1968)   (1869-1925)   (1855-1921)   (1870-1928)

Therese Laucheimer   Max Joseph Freund
(1906-1986)   (1897-1937)

Philip Sigfried Freund   Belle Anne Dwoskin
(Born 1931)   (Born 1937)

Margarette L. (Al Yee)   Mark J.   Perry M.   Jacqueline M.
                          (Laura M. Collins)   (Craig S. Fassbender)

Rachel E. Toepfer   Mathew M.
Christopher S. Toepfer   Philip A. Freund   Freund   Joseph M. Fassbende
Rebecca T. Yee   Samuel S. Fassbender
                                                               Daniel T. Fassbender

54412061R10067

Made in the USA
Columbia, SC
30 March 2019